Suddenly Widowed

A Memoir of Survival

PATTY SLUPECKI

Sandy —
Thank you for
supporting me along
my journey! — Patty

Suddenly Widowed: A Memoir of Survival

Copyright © 2018 by Patty Slupecki

All rights reserved.

ISBN: 978-0-692-14557-9

DEDICATION

This book is dedicated to my family and friends who have supported me over the last 16 years. Some of you have been permanent fixtures in my life and others were passing through. Whether I call you friend or family, I believe you were placed in my life for a reason and am grateful for you. I thank you for the support you offered, the love you gave, the time you shared, the lessons you taught, and the challenges you brought. I am the strong, healthy, independent, happy woman I am today, in part, because you traveled the journey with me.

FREE BONUS MATERIAL

How to Help the Grieving
A Checklist for Family, Friends, Neighbors, and Coworkers

Get exclusive insights and practical information for helping when someone experiences the death of a loved one.

- ✓ Learn what to say and what NOT to say.

- ✓ Understand what is helpful and what is harmful.

- ✓ Overcome the uncomfortableness that surrounds death.

- ✓ Gain confidence with funeral etiquette.

To download the Free Bonus Checklist, visit:

WWW.PATTYSLUPECKI.COM/BONUSMATERIAL

Join Patty Slupecki's Social Community

www.pattyslupecki.com
f @pattyslupecki
t @pattyslupecki

CONTENTS

ACKNOWLEDGMENTS

Throughout the process of writing this book, several individuals offered significant support and encouragement. I'd like to express my gratitude to all those who cheered me on from far and near, offered comments, shared stories, listened to me when I needed to talk things out, and assisted in the editing, proofreading, and design.

I want to acknowledge two people in particular for their unwavering dedication to this project and to me. First, this memoir was made possible by the professional and personal guidance of my wonderful editor, mentor, and friend, Teresa Boyer, of Provisional Pen Writing Services. Second, I was able to finish this book in seven short months because of my exceptionally talented assistant, Linda Jones, who organized, planned, and ran my life so I could focus solely on completing this book.

Lastly, thank you to my book launch team – without you the details of getting this book to my audience would have been overwhelming.

CHAPTER 1
SUNDAY MORNING, SEPTEMBER 8, 2002

"Always say 'goodbye.' Always say 'I love you.' One day, it will be the last moment you share with a loved one. Be sure you can look back on it with a smile." – Patty Slupecki

Wearing the same clothes I put on more than 24 hours earlier, I was happy to pull back into my own driveway. The black Jeep, still hot from the morning sun, came to a stop in my normal parking spot inside the garage. I reached over to my right side, pushed the gearshift into park and turned off the ignition. Just for a moment, I rested my head back on the leather seat and let out an audible sigh of relief; I was home. It was mid-morning on a beautiful September Sunday, and I was looking forward to hugging my kids and kissing my husband after the ordeal I'd just lived through.

I was exhausted and sweaty after entertaining 100 kids, who didn't belong to me, all night long in the unusually high temperature. I had overseen an overnight youth group experience at the zoo. The teenage helpers, four girls and two boys, had planned an animal themed scavenger hunt that crisscrossed the entire property. It felt like I had walked 20 miles chasing after those energetic, excited children who had a tendency to run in every direction.

The air was still thick, sticky, and uncomfortable when the sun went down, and it seemed to take an excessive amount of time for campers and chaperones to settle in for the night. I tried to remain patient with the last few requests of the evening before I turned off the lights and headed into the basement of the old stone building where zoo staffers routinely slept during overnight camps. It was cooler to sleep in one of the administrative offices located on the lower level and was a floor away from all the kids who undoubtedly would be up talking for hours.

In the small office, I was able to stretch out my weary body on a hard, narrow cot which I had set up earlier in the day. Too tired to even change clothes, I was relieved to be off my sore feet and slightly swollen ankles. Finally, all was quiet, and I could close my eyes. Finally, I could let my muscles relax and get some sleep.

Bzzzzz! The deafening sound of the fire alarm jolted me right off the warm cot and onto the cold cement floor. I had to shake off the disorientation I felt from being woken up in such a jarring manner. My mom mode kicked in and an adrenalin rush took over my body. I grabbed my radio to contact security and ran, taking the stairs two at a time, to reach the floor occupied by the other zoo staff. This was no easy task for my five feet two-inch stature, but I had to ensure all the camp leaders were following evacuation protocol to clear the building of frightened campers and panicked parents. My heart was racing; my breathing was shallow and rapid. The words 'just get everyone out' swirled in my mind, over and over and over.

After rushing 100 wide-eyed campers out of the historic building and onto the warm cement of the outdoor walkway, I gathered with parents and chaperones, waiting for information about what was happening. We hadn't been outside more than two minutes when the steady voice of a male security officer came across my handheld radio. "All clear." The radio blared. "False alarm. You may return to the building."

Initially, I was relieved that there was no fire or other emergency. Then, a feeling of annoyance started creeping in. I'm sure I must have rolled my eyes thinking about how long it was going to take to get everyone back into the building and settled down again. It was the exasperated feeling of trying to get your own kids to go to bed and stay there, only I wasn't just dealing with my own two children, I was dealing with 100 children!

Unquestionably, there would be some scared little kids or half-blind parents that would require the lights on in order to navigate their way back to the sleeping bags and yoga mats that were scattered across the first floor of the old stone building. There would be children who needed to use the restroom or want a drink of water. Certainly, there would be more questions asked, questions I had myself, but no answers were available. All I wanted was to sleep, but that was not looking very promising.

Indeed, sleep did not come for me or for many others. We were all happy to see the morning sun rise. With the light of day came the anticipation of packing up our belongings and heading home. A hot, black cup of coffee was nearly in sight.

I was greeted at the door by our big, black Labrador, Bo. His tail was banging with excitement against the side of the washing machine. I gave him a reassuring pat on the head and yelled into the house, "Hello, I'm home." My grip on my small overnight bag loosened and the bag hit the floor with a thud. My enthusiastic, red-headed, four-year-old boy came running around the corner. He jumped into my arms, nearly knocking my worn-out body off balance. His arms and legs wrapped tightly around me as I scooped him up. "Mommy!" he squealed. Jake seemed delighted to have me back home, and he promptly announced that his Daddy had made breakfast.

I leaned over and set Jake back down on the wood floor; he raced off back to his Thomas the Tank Engine train set. I heard Mark call from the kitchen, asking about my night. My sluggish body moved through the house into the kitchen where Mark stood, an entire foot taller than me. He had to bend way over to give me a kiss as I stretched up on my tippy toes to meet him. "Coffee?" he asked. I finally held the cup of caffeine I had been waiting for and sat down on a short stool at the kitchen counter work space we added the year before.

Praising the liquid in my favorite blue jean colored coffee cup, I admired my husband's thoughtful gesture and his biceps that popped out from under his short-sleeved tee.

"You won't believe the night I had," I exclaimed and began to share the story of my action-packed night at the zoo. My voice was louder than usual, and I spoke at a faster pace describing the heat, humidity, miles walked, and the fire alarm going off for no apparent reason. Mark listened intently and topped off my coffee when my cup neared empty.

"What did you do with the kids last night?" I asked. With a devilish grin on his face, Mark explained how he and the kids had enjoyed an evening of doing things that Mommy didn't allow. I shook my head as he described the ice cream flavors they had each chosen for their dinner. Yes, dinner. "Jake picked the blue, red, yellow, and green superman ice cream and it melted down the front of his white shirt like a rainbow," he proudly reported, making it sound much worse than it probably was, all for effect.

He continued, "Ellie ordered a hot fudge sundae with extra cherries on top so she could practice tying knots in the cherry stems with her tongue." "Of course, she did," I said. Our daughter was the most precocious 10-year-old I've ever known. "We ordered pizza for dessert and we ate it on the couch while we watched *Toy Story*."

Mark was really pushing my buttons. He was famous for yanking my chain a little, and he was taking full advantage of the opportunity to see if he could get me riled up. I was envisioning greasy pizza fingers touching my couch cushions and the coffee table. I cringed inside but tried not to give Mark the satisfaction of knowing he was successfully getting to me. It was a well-known fact that eating anywhere except at the kitchen table was never permitted on my watch.

Moments later, my blood was pumping, and the caffeine had taken affect; I was wide awake now but feeling grimy from the night at the zoo. All I wanted was a long shower and some clean clothes. Mark must have sensed this and made me a generous offer: "Go shower. Take your time. I'll take the kids with me and run some errands."

I reminded him that Ellie had a birthday party to attend that afternoon and we still needed to pick up a gift and card for the birthday girl. Mark assured me he could handle it with Ellie's guidance. I was a bit skeptical, worried he would spend too much money on a kid's present, or worse, not spend enough. I was also trying to remember if there was appropriate wrapping paper or maybe a gift bag in the house, but again, Mark said he would take care of it. I was grateful for the time alone to shower and regroup.

I climbed the stairs and headed down the hallway toward Ellie's room. When I reached the doorway, I could see her searching through her dresser drawers. "Hi Ellie. I hear you had ice cream for dinner," I said. Her head turned toward the doorway where I was standing. "Hi Mom. When did you get home?" she asked, trying to deflect my question. "Just a little while ago," I replied and continued.

"Where did you eat your pizza last night?" I was getting pleasure out of baiting her. I wanted to see her squirm just a little.

"Can I wear this bathing suit to Hannah's party?" she asked, completely ignoring my inquiry. I smiled and thought to myself, 'Wow, that is so sweet. She is protecting her dad from getting into trouble for abandoning my rules while I was out of the house.' I stopped asking questions and we discussed what she needed to take to the pool party.

After a few minutes, Mark appeared at the door. "Hey Ellie, let's go get a present for Hannah. Can you help me pick it out, so Mom can stay home and take a shower?" "Sure," she replied. "I know just what I want to get her. A Groovy Girl." They continued their conversation about what they needed to buy at the store and exactly what stores they would go to.

Jake's bedroom was right next door. I popped my head in to tell him what we all were planning to do. He was on his knees, leaning across the white train table, laying out a new track formation. I asked if he wanted to go shopping with Daddy and Ellie, as if there was any real choice. Jake always chose to be with Daddy when he could. I didn't mind that one bit; I thought it was really sweet how close they were.

Mark took charge of Jake's bath time from the time he was born. Now, as a preschooler, Jake loved a challenge from his dad. Every night at bath time, they followed the same routine. Mark would announce, "It's time to race!" Jake would drop whatever he was doing and immediately line up with Mark in the kitchen. They would meet where the carpeting of the family room met the wood floor of the kitchen. Jake would wait patiently, one foot in front of the other, bent at the waist, prepared to rocket himself off to a fast start.

"Ready, set, go!" Mark would yell, and the two of them would begin running through the kitchen, down the hall, around the corner, and up the stairs to the kids' bathroom. As Mark and Jake would hit the stairs in this nightly race, Bo would gallop toward them and, catching Mark, he would begin to grab at his ankles, tail still wagging.

Bo stood eye-to-eye with Jake and was very protective of him. If Bo had the slightest sense that anyone was a threat to Jake, he would insert his hundred-pound body into their path, growl, and show off his massive open jaw. Jake knew Bo would help him win the race.

During these races, screaming, giggling, and the thunderous sound of four legs and four paws pounding up the stairs at once could be heard throughout the house. It was the sound of pure joy and excitement. I loved hearing them race; it always made me smile. The pattern never changed.

So, off they went, Mark, Ellie, and Jake to run their errands and shop for the birthday gift. After they left, I took a long, cool shower and dressed in a pair of clean blue jean shorts and a white tee that were appropriate for the hot day. All the sweaty grime and stress from the night before were gone and I felt refreshed. I even had a renewed level of energy and was ready to enjoy the day with my family.

This Sunday was a typical weekend day with very low-key plans. Mark would fiddle around in the garage or yard, or maybe 'fix' something around the house after he ran or rode his bike. I would take my time prepping some daytime snacks and a favorite recipe or two. We would cook out on the grill for dinner later that evening. I always enjoyed the leisurely pace of cooking for my family on the weekends.

Jake would bounce from 'helping' Mark outside, to checking in with me in the kitchen, and then on to playing with his treasured train set. Ordinarily, Ellie would be playing in her room with her collection of American Girl Dolls or Groovy Girls, but today she would be attending the birthday pool party. It was to be a quiet, peaceful, uneventful Sunday.

About an hour later, I heard the garage door open and the sound of the tags that hung from Bo's collar jingling together as he ran to greet whoever was coming in the back door. My family was home, we were all together, and I felt happy and content.

Jake came running into the house, proudly showing off the new stuffed Scooby-Doo dog that Mark bought him at the store. I rolled my eyes, knowing Mark couldn't say "no" to a request from this cute, warm-hearted little boy. Inside, my heart melted just a bit because of that very thing.

Ellie talked a mile a minute, describing the shopping experience with Daddy and showed me the great gift she picked out for her friend. She was very excited to give her gift away. They also managed to pick out a nice gift bag and card, both selections I approved of.

Mark was a dedicated runner and triathlete. He kept spiral bound journals with the details of every run/ride/swim, time, split, heart rate, and blood sugar level. He was also an insulin dependent diabetic, which necessitated long formulas figuring out grams of sugar needed for the physical output. I'm not sure that even makes sense to you mathematicians, because frankly, math is not my thing, and I never really understood what Mark was doing with all those numbers. But it was important to him and it kept his blood sugar, for the most part, stable when he ran.

Running was a daily commitment for Mark. On the weekends, when he had more time and a flexible schedule, he would do his longer runs and weather and circumstances permitting would take the kids along with him. I remember the first Father's Day after Ellie was born. 3-month-old Ellie gave him a pink, three wheeled, jogging stroller so she could go on runs with her dad. My thinking was, 'I'm home all day alone with this baby and you are not going to arrive home and promptly leave for an hour long run!' I was going to ensure I finagled some alone time for myself with this Father's Day gift! Funny thing is, that was probably Mark's favorite gift ever.

This weekend was no different; Mark was planning to go for a long bike ride as he was training for another triathlon. You know, swim, bike, run some crazy distance for fun! Often, Ellie would ride her bike along with Mark when he ran, and Jake would ride along and nap in the jogging stroller – no, not the pink one. When Jake came along, we purchased a newer blue jogger that had two seats!

On this particular Sunday, Ellie wouldn't be riding along because of the birthday party she was attending, and Jake wanted to ride on the trail bike with his dad. The trail bike is a one wheeled bike with a seat, pedals, and a long, curved bar that attaches onto the stem of an adult's bike. Ours was yellow and Jake could sit on the bike seat, hold on to his own handlebars, and peddle when and if he wanted to. Jake always thought his peddling was helping Mark and he was proud of that.

Mark prepared for his ride. He filled a couple bottles full of orange Gatorade and set them inside the refrigerator to stay cold until he left. I checked the temperature; it was near 90 degrees, clear blue sky, and lots of burning sunshine coming down. Mark planned to be gone for a couple hours, and I began to worry that it was too hot and too long of a ride for Jake. I was also concerned that he would get sunburned during those peak hours of the day. Actually, I was never a fan of Mark taking Jake out on that trail bike. Jake was only four years old, and I was afraid Mark would ride too fast and Jake could fall off. They both always wore helmets, but that didn't ease my over protective mom imagination.

I went up to our room where Mark was changing into his bike shorts and riding shirt and shared my concern with him. As usual, he thought I was being unnecessarily worried and told me everything would be just fine. It was a good thing that Mark was relaxed about life and parenting because I did enough worrying for the both of us. We balanced one another out in that manner; it was a good partnership. I wasn't so sure he was right, but I left the room and went back downstairs all the while trying to think of another reason Jake should stay home with me.

In the meantime, Ellie got her gift all ready to give. She placed it inside the gift bag and asked for my help to make the tissue paper look pretty in the bag. She packed her arsenal of swimming necessities, and I double-checked to be sure she had everything she needed. I also insisted that I help her put the first layer of sunscreen on before she left the house. I didn't trust she could coat herself as well as I could. It was a bit unusual to be having a swim party in September in the Midwest, but this was the perfect weather for a pool party and the birthday girl just happened to have a pool.

"Daddy," Ellie yelled. "Where are you?" She wanted to give him a kiss goodbye before she left. "Up here" he responded from the second floor. Ellie ran up the steps to where his voice was coming from. Why is it that kids always run wherever they go? She said her goodbye and hopped back downstairs.

"I'm taking Ellie to her party and I'll be right back" I said to Mark from the bottom of the staircase. "If you leave before I get back, be sure to put sunscreen on Jake." I knew it would only take me about five minutes to drop Ellie off and make my way back home. I was betting the boys would still be home, so I could see them off as I so often did. Plus, I was still hoping Jake wouldn't go.

I drove Ellie to the party and reminded her that I would be picking her up when the party ended. As a somewhat neurotic, overprotective, safety-conscious young mother, I always told my children that I would never send anyone else to pick them up without letting them know first. I didn't go so far as to set up a code word and in retrospect I can't imagine why I didn't put that into place. I was a fan of teaching my kids every safety precaution I could come up with or heard about on the evening news, including how to escape from the inside of a car trunk, fight off an unfamiliar adult, and run away from a gun in a zigzag pattern. I laugh at my ridiculous self now, but at the time I was dead serious!

I dropped off Ellie and walked her into the backyard of the party house. I wanted to be certain there were plenty of adults there to supervise the kids in the pool. I was satisfied with the situation I encountered, said goodbye, and went directly back home. I was happy to return home before Mark and Jake left, and the few minutes in the car had given me time to create another, better reason to keep Jake home with me. I decided I would bribe him! I didn't make bribing my children a regular practice but saved it for when I really wanted them to conform with my wishes without any negotiations.

The boys were in the garage when I pulled my Jeep into the driveway. Mark went back inside but left the door open, so I knew he would be right back out. I knew this was my chance. I exited my car quickly, approached Jake and said in a very excited tone, "Hey Jake, I have a great idea! If you stay home with me while Daddy goes for a bike ride, we can bake a chocolate cake together."

This was a pretty big deal in our house. I am not a baker and rarely offer any opportunities for the kids to help make a sweet treat. If there is measuring and following directions involved, I'm out. In addition, with Mark being a diabetic, we rarely had sweets of any kind in the house at all. So you can see why a preschooler living in this sugar deprived home would be delighted to stay and bake a chocolate cake with me.

"Really?" Jake's excited little voice asked. I confirmed the promise, adding that he could frost the first piece to seal the deal. Jake was literally jumping with excitement when Mark walked back into the garage. "Mommy is baking a chocolate cake and I get to help. I get the first really big piece!" Jake reported, stretching his arms wide to show just how big his piece of cake was going to be.

Mark shot me that all knowing look from across the garage and shook his head with a smile. My smiling face conveyed to him that I was checking off a little win for myself. We often enjoyed a little nonverbal bantering back and forth; it was all in good fun.

"Come on Mom, let's go," Jake said as he took ahold of my hand and led me toward the kitchen. I followed along, passing Mark on the way, trying to wink at him. I can't wink without contorting my entire face, so it was just one of those things I did to get a laugh out of my family. Mark winked back, a perfect, unobtrusive, effortless wink, as if to chalk one up for himself. We both laughed.

"Tell me when you leave," I ordered Mark.

Jake and I headed into the kitchen and began gathering the necessary tools and ingredients we needed to begin our baking adventure. "We need a measuring cup from that cupboard" I said as I pointed to the bottom cabinet below the coffee maker. Jake would be able to locate and reach that, I thought. He was genuinely thrilled to be helping. Just then, Mark appeared from around the corner. He had come in to give Jake one more chance to go for a bike ride with him. "Okay, I'm ready to go. I can still attach your bike if you want to peddle along with me, Jake," he said. I looked at Jake and silently mouthed the words 'chocolate cake' ensuring Mark would be able to see me. Jake stayed home.

Mark kissed Jake on the top of the head and said, "Okay, have fun baking your cake with Mommy. I'll see you later Bud. Love ya."

I was leaning my left hip on the counter, my weight balanced on my right foot. Mark approached, and I stretched to give him a big squeeze and kiss. He said, "I'll only be gone a couple hours. I love you." "Love you too," I said. It was about 11 am when he headed out the door. As I always did, I hollered after him, "Be careful."

That was the last time I saw Mark alive. It was the last time I kissed him goodbye. It was the last time I hugged him. It was the last time I heard and said, 'I love you.' It was the last chocolate cake I ever baked.

CHAPTER 2
THE PHONE CALL

"People, things, and situations are put in front of us to serve a purpose. Be open to receiving a message or a lesson." – Patty Slupecki

There was a heavenly aroma filling the air as Jake and I removed the chocolate cake from the oven and placed it on the cooling rack to rest. Jake excitedly asked if we could eat it. "It's too hot right now, we have to let it cool down first," I replied.

It was just after noon and the lack of sleep was catching up with me. My eyes were feeling heavy, and my energy was zapped after cleaning up the kitchen. Thinking how well my first baking bribe worked, I gave Jake another very special offer. "If you will lay on the couch with me, you can watch any movie you want," I explained. "When the movie ends, the cake will be cool enough to frost." "Can we eat it then?" Jake asked. I quickly confirmed.

Bait taken. Jake chose his movie; *Toy Story* or maybe it was *Toy Story 2*. Jake loved these movies and would watch them over and over again. I think he could recite most of the dialogue from both movies.

I appreciate the adult humor infused into most of the Disney movies. It allowed me to tolerate watching them repeatedly. *Toy Story* was my favorite too.

"Can I put the movie in?" Jake asked, waving the VHS tape above his head. Remember how much space all those tapes took up? The bookshelves in our family room held no fewer than 100 movies and kids' TV shows, I'm sure.

"Go ahead," I told Jake. He pushed the tape into the player with one finger as if he were a magician performing a show stopping trick. My exhausted arms could barely close the family room curtains to keep the bright sun from shining in and causing a glare on the TV screen.

I settled in on one side of the couch and told Jake that I was going to close my eyes for a few minutes. He snuggled in beside me as the movie began. We were both content.

At 2:15 pm I was startled awake. I remember specifically looking at the clock on the wall from where I was lying. I didn't know what startled me, but for some reason the time stuck with me.

I looked at Jake. He was asleep on the other end of the couch. I looked in the direction of the static sound coming from the television. The movie had ended and there were black, gray, and white zigzagged lines dancing across the screen. It took me a second to get my bearings after waking up so abruptly from my nap. I looked at the clock again and wondered why Mark wasn't home.

At first, I was slightly irritated, thinking he probably stopped to talk to a neighbor or was watering bushes in the yard and forgot to tell me he was home, both of which had previously occurred. I was trying to convince myself not to worry.

Jake, having also woken up, came running across the wood floors in his bare feet as I was looking out the front window. He was always barefooted, and I loved to hear the soft sound of his little feet slapping on the floor as he ran through the house. Always running, never walking. He mumbled something about a very important Lego building mission and jumped up the stairs, one step at a time. He had completely forgotten about the chocolate cake waiting on the kitchen counter.

When I glanced back out the window, I still didn't see Mark and decided to walk into the garage. I looked around for Mark's bike, but it wasn't there. I was less worried and a little more annoyed that he hadn't bothered to call and let me know he was going to be home later than expected.

The loud ring of the home phone interrupted my thoughts. I walked over to the kitchen counter where the cordless handset was sitting and looked at the incoming number. I didn't recognize the number but answered the call anyway. The woman's voice on the other end asked, "May I speak with Patty Slupecki, please?" I responded. The woman identified herself and said she was calling from St. Vincent Hospital. She continued on in a very matter-of-fact manner and said that Mark had been in an accident and they would like me to come to the hospital.

I quietly gasped and quickly asked, "Is he okay?" The calm voice simply said, "The doctor will talk to you when you get here. There's no need to rush." This seemed reassuring, so I wasn't too concerned. I also recalled how Mark's brother, Andy, had been in an accident on his bicycle and had a few injuries but completely recovered. This thought was also reassuring to me.

I thanked the woman and continued, "I have two young children and need to get someone to stay with them and then I'll be right over." The woman replied that I could take my time and we ended our call.

For some reason, my mind's eye was picturing Mark sitting on an emergency room rolling gurney, wearing a hospital gown tied only at the back of the neck. He had a broken leg and my imagination went on to worry about how I was going to take care of him with our bedroom and bathroom on the second floor.

I shook my head as if to empty out the crazy contents of an imagination gone wild and decided to take first things first. I had to find someone to come to the house and stay with Jake, and I had to pick up Ellie from her party. As I snapped back to reality, a little bit of panic began to grow; an uncomfortable feeling began creeping into my stomach and chest.

Even as I write this, that feeling is starting to build. It's like a sucker punch to the middle of my diaphragm that leaves an indentation I just can't seem to breathe through. It keeps my torso slightly bent in and tight, shoulders rounded, and my breaths short and shallow. I don't like it.

Realizing that making arrangements for the kids was going to take a bit of time, I called Mark's mom, Pat. She was a nurse, was typically overbearing, and would insert herself into any situation without a thought. These were not my favorite qualities of hers unless it was a medical situation, in which case I relied on her outspoken pushiness to ensure the best care and my understanding of what was going on. I knew she would be the best person to be with Mark until I could get there. She could also get there faster than I could, so Pat was my first phone call.

I had feared because it was a beautiful afternoon she may be out golfing and not at home. We had cell phones back then, but they were not the primary means for calling people. They were more for important or emergency calls. Often, we didn't even keep them on, never thinking there would actually be a reason for someone to call our cell number.

I dialed my mother-in-law's home number and was relieved when she answered right away. Not letting her get a word in, I blurted out that Mark had been in an accident. I then continued on in one breath, "He was on his bike, and they want me to come to the hospital - I have to get someone to stay with Jake - Ellie is at a pool party and I still have to figure out how to get her home - Can you go to the hospital right now, so Mark isn't alone? I'll be there as fast as I can."

Pat replied that of course she would go and asked which hospital Mark was sent to. "St. V's," I answered. "I'll meet you there." And I hung up the phone.

My second call was to my mom, Mary. Thankfully, she answered right away too. Already tired of telling the story, I gave her a breathless rundown on what was going on and pleaded with her to come over and stay with Jake. She would have never said anything other than yes! "I'll drive you to the hospital," she said. I insisted that I would be fine and that I just needed her to be here with Jake. "Pat is calling back, I have to go." I switched lines and answered the incoming call.

"Are you sure you have the right hospital? Did you mean St. Anne's instead of St. Vincent? I'm going over there. It's closer and they would have taken him to the closest hospital," Pat announced. "No." I replied. "The woman called from St. V's; I'm sure. Please go to St. V's right away."

The call was interrupted. This time, it was my mom calling back. I switched the phone line again, beginning to feel annoyed with the calls and clarifications. I just kept thinking that I needed to get to the hospital and didn't need the constant questioning.

"Hi Mom," I answered the call. She began, "I called Sue, (my sister) she's on her way to your house now. I also called Uncle, (my mom's brother, John, known to us as simply Uncle). He is on his way to pick you up and drive you to the hospital." She continued, "I'll come stay with Jake until Sue gets there, and then I'll come to the hospital with you."

Unwilling to argue I replied that her plan was fine with me. I remember thinking it was odd that everyone was making such a big deal out of this. It was simpler to just go along with the plan.

I still had to get Ellie, but she would be very disappointed if I made her leave the party early. She was a 10-year-old girl, and I could just imagine the long, drawn-out scene she would create. There would be tears and begging for one more jump in the pool, one more piece of birthday cake, one more game. I could not be delayed by that kind of preteen drama. Besides, there was really no reason to cut short her fun with friends if I could find another solution.

Wondering what to do, given the fact that I had always told the kids that I would never send anyone else to pick them up without telling them ahead of time, I decided to call one of the other moms, Annette. Ellie knew her well because we were in the same carpool together for school and Annette's daughter, Cayley was at the party too. I figured Ellie would trust her and ride home with her when the party was over.

I called Annette, told her that Mark had been in an accident, and asked her to please bring Ellie home. She responded, "Of course, I will. Does she know to ride home with me?"

"No," I said. "That's what worries me." Annette assured me that Ellie would leave the party with her and get home safely. I quickly thanked her and hung up the phone.

Finally, I went upstairs to talk to Jake. He had Legos dumped out all over the floor of his room, sorted into piles by color and size. "Hey Jake, Wow, it looks like you have a big building project going on." I continued, "Grammy is coming over to play with you for a while. I have to go pick up Daddy. He fell off his bike and needs some help."

Jake was unconcerned with me leaving and I was relieved. I didn't want him to worry. "Yippy!" He yelled. He was very pleased that Grammy was coming over. She was always a very welcome visitor and would cooperate with his every wish.

My imagination took over my conscious thoughts once again, and I decided I should put on a pair of sneakers as they would be more sensible than flip-flops if I had to help Mark get into the car. Next, I decided I should put the contents of my purse into my small, black and white checked backpack. This would allow me to have both hands free to help Mark, and I wouldn't have to worry about leaving my purse anywhere. Plus, it would match my plain white tee.

The front door was open, and I was standing there watching out the glass storm door for my Mom to arrive. From the end of my short street, I saw a car rounding the corner. As the car sped down the cul-de-sac, I could see that it was Annette. She left her car in the street right in front of my house and rushed up to my front door.

Her keys jingled from the key ring she held in one hand. In the other hand, she held an overstuffed wallet. As she reached the front porch, she tossed them both into the corner of the front stoop. She came through the door, threw her arms around me and squeezed tightly. "What can I do?" she asked. I thought she was overreacting but thanked her and said how much I appreciated her picking up Ellie for me.

As we were standing there, Uncle arrived. He had to maneuver around Annette's randomly parked car to pull into the driveway. My mom immediately followed.

On his way into the house, Uncle picked up the keys and wallet from the porch. He held them up in the air and asked, "Who left their things outside? It probably isn't a good idea to leave them out there." Annette thanked him, claimed her belongings, and headed out to pick up the girls from the birthday party.

When my mom reached the front door, Uncle took charge, "Mary, you stay here and get things settled. I'll take Patty to the hospital." My mom approved of the plan and gave me a hug. "We'll be just fine here. I'll see you soon."

I don't know why I remember this part of the story at all, let alone in so much detail. But it is clearly etched in my memory, and I felt compelled to share it here.

It seemed like everyone was making a big deal out of the situation, which was highly unusual. I had made a handful of trips to the hospital over the last few years as most parents of young children do. I never had an entourage like this before. In hindsight, I believe there was another power at work providing me with the support I was going to need.

Uncle drove me straight down Bancroft Street to St. Vincent Hospital. I remember him talking during the car ride, but I don't remember anything about the conversation. I do remember having a light-headed feeling, wondering what was waiting for me as I looked out the window at the passing landscape. The 10 or 15-minute drive seemed to take so much longer.

We turned left into the emergency room entrance and were greeted by a security guard. He was an older gentleman wearing a blue uniform with the hospital insignia on his right shoulder. Uncle rolled down the passenger side window so we could speak to the guard.

"I was called to come to the emergency room. My husband was in an accident," I told the guard. "Okay. You'll have to park on the other side." The guard pointed off in the other direction.

"Patty, you get out here and go on in. I'll park and be in right behind you," Uncle said. I don't remember saying anything else. I just got out of the car and the guard closed the door behind me and pointed me toward the ER entrance.

I walked through two large, automated glass doors that slid open when I approached. My eyes darted around the open area and I located a desk that seemed to be a registration area. A big, dark skinned man, dressed in all white stood to greet me. I approached the desk and explained to the man that someone, I couldn't remember her name, from the hospital had called me because my husband had been in accident. That was all I said.

The man came around to the front of the desk, gestured in a far-off direction, and said, "Follow me, please." 'Wow,' I thought. 'That was odd. He didn't even ask my name.'

I followed the figure dressed in white, past a few other people sitting in the open ER area, to a closed door in the back corner of the waiting room. "You can wait in this room ma'am," he said in a kind voice. "I'll go tell the doctor you are here. He'll be right in to talk to you."

When the man opened the door and held it for me, I could see my mother-in-law standing in the middle of the room all by herself. I walked into the small space, our eyes met, and she wrapped her arms around me. Not a single word was said, but somehow, I just knew. Mark was dead.

.

CHAPTER 3
THE WAITING ROOM

"You can withstand much more than you ever thought possible. Yes, you can!"
– Patty Slupecki

My knees began to buckle. I felt all the strength and structure that held my body upright escape. I was going to fall. "I have to sit down." I told Pat. She released her grip on me and I sank, nearly lifeless, into the dark leather sofa that sat along one side of the private waiting room.

A feeling of numbness came over my body and my mind went completely blank. My entire physical, mental, and spiritual being was in a trauma induced state of shock. I didn't have a single thought in my head. I didn't have a question to ask. I didn't even have a tear to shed in that moment. My world went dark.

The details and events that occurred from this point on are sketchy at best in my mind. I have many holes in my memory around this event and have relied on others to fill the gaps for me. Occasionally, a memory returns, but for the most part, I lost an entire year of my life.

"They wouldn't tell me anything," Pat said, out of breath. "They wouldn't let me see him. I knew something was wrong. I was told I would have to wait until you arrived, and the doctor spoke to you first because you are his wife. That's when I knew." Being a nurse, Pat was well aware of hospital protocol. "I screamed at them, is my son dead?" She continued, "That's when they told me."

The waiting room door opened, and an unfamiliar woman entered. She was rather short and a bit stocky. Her brown hair was cut close to her head and tucked behind her ears. A simple cross hung from a long chain around her neck and rested on her conservative clothing. Behind the simple woman was a familiar face completely out of context. It was Beth, the school nurse at my children's elementary school. 'Why would she be here? Did she know I was here? Did she know about Mark?' I wondered, completely confused.

Beth didn't say anything. She closed the door behind her and stood to the side of the room, looking at me with no expression. The first woman approached me and held her hand out for me to shake. "Hello Mrs. Slupecki. My name is Clara, and I'm from Pastoral Care here at the hospital. I was the one who spoke to you on the phone." She explained and proceeded to sit down on the matching leather couch directly across from where I sat in the narrow room.

"I'm sorry to tell you that your husband, Mark, was involved in an accident this afternoon and died as a result of his injuries. The doctors did everything they could, but Mark's injuries were too severe," Clara said. Suddenly my mother-in-law interrupted and demanded to know what happened.

I just looked at Clara; I was motionless, speechless, and physically weak. She continued her report. "It seems, while riding his bicycle, he was struck by a pickup truck at the intersection of Bancroft and the Fulton County line. The driver stopped and waved down the first approaching car." Clara pointed over to the corner of the room where Beth was standing motionless. "Beth and her daughter were the first ones that stopped to help and called 911."

My mind could simply not absorb the words I was hearing; in fact, I'm sure I didn't even hear most of the words she said at all. I wasn't sitting comfortably on the cold couch; I was perched on the edge of the seat cushion, feet on the floor, slumped over, my arms leaning on my legs to hold my body upright. It was all I could do to keep myself from melting into the huge, black hole that was waiting to swallow me.

When I was able to raise my eyelids again and look up, the room was filled with people. I slowly moved my eyes from person to person. I was all alone on the big couch but across the room beyond Clara and Pat I saw Uncle, my mom, and next to Beth was a thin woman in hospital scrubs wearing a name badge that identified her as an RN. I don't remember any of them entering the room. They were just suddenly there.

"Mrs. Slupecki, the doctor that was with your husband on the life helicopter was called out on another emergency flight, but the doctor who worked on your husband when he arrived will be in to talk to you in just a few minutes," the nurse told me. I shook my head enough to acknowledge that I understood.

The next thing I can remember is the doctor kneeling on the floor in front of me with his hands covering mine. He was kind, gentle, and spoke to me in a soft voice. He talked to me, but I have absolutely no idea what he said. I can recall staring into his eyes, hoping he was going to fix everything. I saw his lips move but didn't hear his words. He stayed there, kneeling on the hard, institutional flooring for a long time. I think he could feel my pain. I didn't want him to leave me, and I think it was difficult for him to break away. We both knew, without words, that when he left that room he would take with him my last hope for a different outcome, and life as I knew it would be gone forever.

Clara and the nurse left along with the young ER doctor. To this day, I don't know that doctor's name, and I sometimes wonder if he remembers that moment we spent together. I think the experience we shared stole a little piece of him that day too.

A telephone sat on an end table on the other side of the room. Uncle picked up the receiver and dialed his home number to report the news to my aunt, Abby. He told her that he was at the hospital with me, and then holding the receiver away from his face, he looked at me and said, "Brace yourself, this is going to be the first time you hear someone say this."

He continued his conversation with Aunt Abby. "Mark was killed," he said.

The others in the room took turns making the necessary, immediate phone calls. When Clara returned to the room, she looked at me and said, "The hospital needs you to positively identify the body." My heart fell to the pit of my stomach. "The nurse will be back in a minute to explain what you are going to see and what to expect."

"NO. I can't." I said. "Yes, you can, and we will all be with you," she replied in a gentle yet commanding tone.

Everyone was quiet when the nurse returned. We all gave our attention to her and listened carefully. "When you go into the room, you will see Mark's body covered with a white sheet. The only part of him you will see is his head. Don't move the sheet. You don't want to look under it," she instructed.

My eyes must have doubled in size and the color drained from my face because Uncle rushed to my side and held onto my arm as if I might collapse. The nurse continued, "There is a tube in his nose and a tube in his mouth. They are no longer connected to anything, but because there was an accident, the coroner requires the tubes be left in place. You will also see some gauze pads across his forehead. Don't move those either."

Panic escalated throughout my body. "Do you have any questions before you go in?" asked the nurse. I couldn't utter a sound and no one else voiced a question. I was terrified, shaking; I did not want to do this.

"We're ready," Clara told the nurse. The first tears began to well in my eyes as Uncle helped me to my feet. I was not given a choice.

The nurse opened the waiting room door and said, "Follow me, please." Still holding onto my arm, Uncle said, "I've got Patty. Mary, hold on to Pat." My mom complied although I'm certain it killed her not being the one holding on to me. She has never told me that; it's not her style. I just know it.

When everyone was through the doorway, the nurse continued down a very bright, sterile hallway in silence. We passed several open doorways that revealed empty rooms and a nurses station where several people dressed in scrubs were gathered around a chart. They were talking in a normal conversational tone. No one looked up as we walked by. Uncle and I were behind the nurse, my mom and mother-in-law fell in line behind us, and Beth and Clara remained a few steps back.

We finally stopped in front of a wide doorway only identified by the number 7 on the wall next to the opening. There was a green and blue patterned curtain drawn to hide the contents of the room. "This is the room," said the nurse. "I'll move the curtain and you can go in."

The sound of the curtain hooks sliding through the track on the ceiling were almost deafening to my ears. Once pulled back, Uncle hesitated for a moment and then led me past the curtain, or maybe he pulled me, alongside Mark's lifeless body. I very gently touched his shoulder through the white sheet as if I were concerned I may hurt his injured body.

My mom and Pat stood on the other side of the hospital bed as Pat started to cry, holding her hand over her mouth. I looked at Mark's face; he looked normal to me. Yes, there were the tubes and gauze, but his face wasn't swollen, his lips weren't blue, and I didn't see any blood. His eyes were closed, and he didn't look like he was in any pain or discomfort. He looked like he was taking a nap. I thought to myself 'how can he be dead; his face looks the same as when I saw him earlier today?'

I suppose that was denial, or perhaps naïveté regarding dead bodies. I had experienced the death of grandparents, but I was much more removed. In each case, I only saw the body laid out in a casket at the funeral home. There were always plenty of people around, snacks in the private family area, and out-of-towners that were fun to visit with. It seemed more acceptable because I viewed my grandparents as old and sick and their death was, to some degree, anticipated.

I think I was holding my breath, afraid to move as I stood beside Mark in disbelief. All of a sudden, I felt sick to my stomach. I asked for the restroom and started out the door and into the hall. The nurse, Beth, and Clara were waiting there. "I'll show you," said the nurse, and quickly led me around the corner to the nearest restroom.

I became physically sick and must have been in the restroom for some time because my mom came, knocking on the door to check on me. "Patty, are you okay? Do you need anything?" she asked.

"I'll be out in a minute," I said. I was glad I thought to put my purse contents into the small backpack. On my back, it was out of my way and I didn't have to put it on the floor. I cleaned myself up, splashed some cold water on my face and opened the restroom door. My mom was standing there waiting for me.

We walked silently back into the room with Mark's body. Pat and Uncle were still standing on the right side of the bed, and the nurse and Clara stood at Mark's feet. I don't know how long we stayed in that room, but eventually Clara broke the silence and suggested, "Why don't you say your goodbyes and we'll go back to the waiting room."

Pat gasped through her tears, gave Mark's arm a light pat through the sheet and said goodbye. I watched as my mom led Pat out of the room. Uncle was standing next to me again, there for support, I'm sure. He bent over and kissed Mark on the head, "Goodbye Mark," he said. I think Uncle sensed my uneasiness and made this gesture to show me it was okay to kiss Mark; it was okay to say goodbye.

But I wasn't just afraid, I was terrified. I don't know why or of what, but I couldn't kiss Mark or touch his bare skin. I choose instead to brush his hair back with my fingers and lightly touch his shoulder again through the sheet covering him.

That is my only regret. I wish I would have been brave enough to kiss him goodbye, to hug and hold him for a last moment. I wish I had known I couldn't hurt his injured body, that he felt no more pain or discomfort. I wish I would have been brave enough to spend those last few moments alone with him. I wish I would have thought to talk to him. I wish I would have held his hand even though it was under the sheet.

Tears welled in my eyes again as I said goodbye to my husband, the father of my children, the love of my life, my best friend, my protector, my biggest supporter. I backed my way out of room number 7 and stopped at the doorway for another minute, still looking at Mark's body just lying there. I was trying to gather the courage to turn away. I didn't want to leave him there alone. Feeling my hesitation and inability to move my feet from that doorway, Uncle said, "Let's go back to the waiting room." He took my arm and we made our way back down the hallway.

When I entered the private waiting room again, I noticed the others sitting around the room on the chairs in the corner and the one couch, but no one was sitting on the couch where I was sitting when my life was shattered. They were chatting in quiet voices but stopped when I walked in. Again, I sat down alone across from Clara. I was alone in my mind, I was alone on the couch, I was alone in the world, yet, I was surrounded by loving, supportive family.

"What do I do now?" I asked Clara. "You go home and tell your children," she replied. I asked how I could do that. "You just say it. The words will come to you," Clara said. I did not find this one bit helpful. How could I possibly 'just tell them'?

Panic surfaced and washed over me again, my heart raced, and I could barely breathe. The thought of having to tell my children, 10-year-old Ellie and 4-year-old Jake, that their Daddy was never coming home again was the worst, all-encompassing feeling I've ever experienced.

I wanted this horrible nightmare to end. I wanted to close my eyes and make it all disappear. I didn't want to deal with it. I didn't want it to be true. I didn't want my kids to be without their Daddy. I didn't want to be without my husband. I wanted my happy, normal family life back. I wanted Mark back.

CHAPTER 4
TELLING THE KIDS

*"When you place your focus outside yourself, the impossible
somehow becomes possible."*
– Patty Slupecki

The ride home from the hospital was a reality check for me as I was transported from the life I knew to a different, undesired and unknown life. I sat in the front passenger seat of my mom's car; it was just the two of us. I'm sure we talked about what to say to the kids when I got home, but I can't remember any of the conversation from that 20-minute commute.

As my mom made the last turn onto the quiet cul-de-sac where my once perfect family of four called home, I took a deep breath. I was filling my lungs for the last time before I dove under the water, below the jagged edges of a coral reef. My mind shut off and locked away my own physical and emotional pain as if I were losing consciousness and entering an out-of-body state. Motherly instincts took over my being. I had to be strong for my children; I needed to reassure them that they, we, would be okay.

I didn't know how we were going to be okay, or even if we would be, but I had to show unshakable certainty to my children. I had to appear as though I knew just what to do. But I didn't know what to do. I didn't have a plan or know what words I would use. My focus was singular, narrowed to my children's well-being and nothing else mattered.

The driveway was already full of cars, so my mom parked in the street in front of my house. I opened the car door without saying anything more and stepped out into my new world. There was no hesitation in my movements. I had blinders on now; I had to get to my children.

I walked purposefully across the front lawn and up the small hill that was suddenly a mountain to my front door. My sister, Sue, had been watching for us to arrive and came rushing outside before I made it to the front porch. She extended her arms out to hug me, crying her condolences. "I can't," I whispered. "I have to get to Jake and Ellie." My spine was rigid and immobile, every muscle in my body tensed as if holding my insides together. I pushed right past her without accepting her hug. I knew I would fall apart if I stopped to acknowledge her sympathy, and I would not let my children see that. I was not going to frighten them.

As I sit here now, reliving these moments, I realize what true love is. This was the worst day of my life. I lost my husband, my family unit, my security, everything that I knew. Yet, none of that surfaced once I stepped out of my mom's car, nor did it matter because my greatest pain was for my children. The trajectory of their lives would be forever altered in ways no one could anticipate or control. The love I had for my children was completely selfless in that moment. I am still awed by and grateful for the ability to love like that.

Before both of my feet crossed the threshold into my home, Ellie was charging through the front hallway to be the first one gaining my attention. At 10 years old, she knew this ordinary Sunday had shifted, something was askew in her world, and she was going to find out what was happening. Ellie always wanted to be 'in the know' and had a way of inserting herself into conversations where she could gather information and get answers. 4-year-old Jake seemed completely unaware that anything was amiss and was too busy playing to greet me. Or maybe he sensed there was something wrong and subconsciously avoided finding out more.

I told Ellie there was something I had to tell her and Jake. The two of us walked together through the house to locate Jake in the family room. Ellie kept firing questions, insistent on gaining more insight as to why I didn't pick her up from the party, why Aunt Sue was at the house without cousin Sophie, and why her Dad wasn't home. By the time I made it into the living room with both kids, the room was full of people. It had only been a few minutes. I hadn't heard or seen anyone arrive. I was exclusively attentive to my children; everything and everyone around the three of us was completely out of focus, a visual blur.

I sat down in the center of the sofa and pulled the kids next to me. Ellie sat on my left, her feet dangling off the front of the sofa where she and her Dad would sit together on their late night ice-cream-eating rendezvous. Jake sat on his knees, curled in close on my right side.

I began talking immediately in a steady voice, not stopping to gather thoughts or search for the right words. I just opened my mouth and the words were there in one unemotional breath. "I have something very sad to tell you. While Daddy was on his bike ride, a pickup truck hit him. A doctor took Daddy to the hospital in a helicopter, and they did everything they could to help Daddy. But he was hurt too badly, and Daddy died." Enough said.

"Nooo!" Ellie wailed, and tears started streaming down her

cheeks. Jake, in a matter-of-fact tone said, "No, he didn't," and climbed off the sofa and left the room. He returned a moment later with a handful of tissues and climbed back into his spot next to me. Jake leaned across me and reached out his arm to wipe the tears from his sister's face.

Time stood still for a while. No more words came to me. I just sat there, holding my children.

CHAPTER 5
JAKE'S FIRST FEATHER

"Acknowledgement of a Higher Power, the Universe, Source, or God brings a level of comfort only available through faith." – Patty Slupecki

Two days after Mark was killed, I was carrying Jake down the stairs at home, his little arms and legs wrapped tightly around me. He was chattering away as he twirled one of my red curls around his finger. I can't remember why I was carrying him; he was four and perfectly capable of walking on his own, but after Mark died Jake was very clingy. He was my little shadow, staying very close to me, and I really didn't want him or Ellie too far out of my sight.

I was afraid to let either of my kids leave the house for fear of something happening to them. I simply could not bear the thought of Jake or Ellie not being with me. I needed them, and their safety and happiness became my obsession and reason for living. Thank God for the loving and supportive family and friends that surrounded us. They surely saved my children from being rolled up in Bubble Wrap and confined to the house until they grew up.

We had only taken a few steps down the stairs when Jake asked why his Daddy hadn't sent him a feather yet. My heart began to sink. In our home, feathers are a message from someone in Heaven. We believe they are a sign that everything is okay up in Heaven and we are okay here on earth. Finding a feather always brings a smile and a small sense of peacefulness.

This is a tremendously comforting belief, one that began for me in the early fall of 1993 when a friend's 15-month-old son, Hunter, passed away suddenly. The day of his funeral, Mike and Liz, Hunter's parents, received a floral arrangement delivered to their home. It was a simple bouquet of fresh, colorful flowers arranged in a clear glass vase.

Liz gasped when the arrangement was handed to her at the front door. Our longtime friend, Brenda, and I inquired who might have sent the arrangement and wondered where the card was. The three of us had been through a lot together over the years, and of course we were together during this tragedy in Liz's life. We were all curious about the mysterious arrangement.

In the center of the pops of orange and yellow blooms stood a single tall feather. Brenda and I looked and could not find a card or any identifying information about where the arrangement came from or who sent it. "We have to find out! We have to know where the feather came from.," we exclaimed.

Liz went on to explain how, years earlier, she had a conversation with a fellow passenger on a cross-country flight. The stranger had shared his belief that feathers were a sign from a loved one in heaven. A feather would be delivered to those left behind, reassuring them all was well after death.

When that feather came into our lives, it connected the three of us on a spiritual level. While we all came from different religious upbringings, our faith in a higher power and our belief in what feathers symbolize cemented an unbreakable bond between us. As I write this, Brenda, Liz and I have been friends for 26 years, and every year we spend a week at the beach together. And yes...we always find feathers!

Before my heart had enough time to sink to the bottom of my stomach or my eyes to fill with tears, I saw it. Perched right on top of Jake's shoulder sat the most perfect curved, white baby feather.

I remember gasping and sitting down ever so gently, halfway down the stairs, so as not to dislodge the perfect placement of Jake's first feather. Jake was now sitting on my lap, looking at me with his questioning, big blue eyes, unaware of what he was about to discover. "Sit very still," I whispered. I took ahold of Jake's light blue tee and pulled it around to the front of his body. I pointed to the feather without saying a word. Jake's face lit up, his eyes doubled in size, and he smiled for the first time since Mark's death.

"Mommy, Daddy sent me a feather!" Jake was almost yelling with excitement. "I knew he was okay up there," Jake said. I asked him what he would like to do with his feather. He immediately proclaimed that he wanted to save it in a special place. I gently plucked the little, white feather from Jake's shoulder and placed it into his cupped hands. He closed his hands ever so slowly as to not cause the slightest damage to that tiny thing.

"Come on," I said. "Let's go find your special place." I lifted Jake to his feet and turned to go back upstairs and Jake followed along. I remembered that I had an old, empty jewelry box in the top dresser drawer in my bedroom. Jake wasn't saying a word; he was just patiently waiting, holding his cupped hands close to his chest. I opened the top drawer, shuffled some things aside, and sure enough in the back of that disorganized drawer was a white, square box left over from some past jewelry gift or purchase.

I lifted the box up in the air exclaiming, "This is the special place. It's a special box where you can collect all the feathers Daddy sends you." I opened the box, removed the square piece of cotton-like padding, and held it out for Jake to place his first feather inside. Slowly, Jake opened his hands, and, with the most careful touch, he picked up the feather and did just that. We put the lid on together.

"You know what we need now?" I asked Jake. "A rubber band. It will hold the lid on tight so the feather won't fall out. Follow me."

I headed down the steps, around the corner, and into the kitchen with Jake directly behind me. I opened the narrow junk drawer next to the dishwasher and pulled out a bobby pin, highlighter, a box of staples, and an extra set of keys. Then I found the perfect sized rubber band to secure Jake's special feather collection box.

Jake held the box tightly with both hands, and I placed the band around it. I could see the sense of peace come over Jake's face, and, for a moment, I shared in that feeling.

CHAPTER 6
THE TROOPS ARRIVE

"Lean on those willing to stand firm for you." – Patty Slupecki

The rawness of my situation left me paralyzed in my very existence. Having the troops gradually move in was a blessing that eased my daily responsibilities. I was lovingly led through the necessary motions and completely relieved of all tasks that could be delegated. Errands, funeral planning, ordering flowers, organizing the funeral lunch, and contacting all the necessary individuals and companies were all handled on my behalf.

My brother-in-law, Mike, and his wife, Sharie, were the first of the troops to arrive. The funeral was planned for a week out because my mom's husband was scheduled for heart surgery three days after Mark's death. The short delay also allowed plenty of time for others to make their travel arrangements from across the country. But immediately, Mike and Sharie were on a flight from their home in Florida to Toledo. After landing, they headed straight to my house and took up residence for the next week or so. I can't imagine what I would have done without them. They stepped in and took over my life at a time when I could only barely breathe.

Mike and I had not been particularly close. There was no reason for this; it was simply circumstantial. We all had young children and were wrapped up in our own busy family lives. Mark was the oldest of three brothers, and Mike is the youngest. The two of them would occasionally have a phone conversation where I would say a simple 'hello' and pass the phone on to Mark. It was just our routine, no hidden meaning.

I grew up with one sister and no brothers, so I didn't understand, nor was I interested in, the weird things guys discussed. Talking about movie lines, video games, and sports was foreign to me. I was more interested in discussing the latest craft ideas, activities to keep the kids busy, and my feelings! Although the brothers and their families spent time together during holidays and special occasions, we naturally split into guy conversations and girl conversations, which left Mike and I with a rather superficial, brother-in-law / sister-in-law kind of relationship.

But something unexpected happened after Mark's death; Mike became my best friend overnight. He was suddenly my confidant and protector. Mark's little brother was now the one I could lean on, the one who could answer my questions and guide me in making decisions. There was no one I trusted and confided in more than Mike. To this day, he remains my go-to guy for all the ups and downs of life.

Sharie, no less helpful, jumped into the family and household tasks as soon as she arrived. She visited our pediatrician, explained the situation, and asked for guidance in helping the kids. Sharie made sure the laundry was done and the kids had clean clothes. She made meals for the kids and tried to coax me into eating a little something. She welcomed visitors and spared me from answering questions and retelling the story over and over again. She made sure the house was picked up and created a spreadsheet to keep track of all the well-wishers.

Mike spent hours in Mark's home office cracking his computer codes and passwords and finding and organizing all the necessary paperwork. He located the insurance policies and investment statements. He put things in order so I would be able to find and access any documents I might need and worked with my sister on a financial plan for me. Both my sister and Mike are CPAs, so they were well suited for this task and made sure the kids and I would be financially secure for the time being.

One evening during that first week, I was tucking Jake into bed in my room. He was used to Mark tucking him in, reading stories, and lying down with him for a while. Jake didn't want to go to bed without his Daddy; I didn't have the energy or desire to fight that battle, so I let him sleep in my bed. Plus, having Jake there made my bedtime a little less lonely.

That evening I heard a rather loud chirping sound as Jake crawled under the covers. The early Fall temperatures had been so comfortable I had been leaving the windows open day and night. At first, I ignored the noise, but as I was reading Jake a bedtime story, the chirping became persistent, almost annoying. I scooted myself off the bed and went to the window where the chirping seemed to be coming from. My plan was to close the window to muffle the sound so Jake could fall asleep.

The chirping stopped when I leaned over Mark's bedside table and began rolling the window inward. Suddenly I noticed a handful of debris, sticks, and some straw tucked into the corner between the window and screen. I briefly wondered how it got there, but I didn't really care. I took a deep breath and blew the debris like it was a candle on a birthday cake. That didn't clear the window, so I took a deeper breath and blew harder. It was much like trying to blow out trick candles that keep reigniting. I was making no progress. I opened the drawer in the bedside table where Mark always kept a small flashlight. Digging through Mark's belongings brought the reality of his death back to the forefront of my mind and an uncomfortable heaviness sank through my body.

When I found the flashlight, I shined the beam of light directly into the window corner. It was then that I could make out the intricate, woven sides of a bird's nest. 'You have got to be kidding me,' I thought. How the hell did a nest get there so fast? This was a problem Mark should solve, not me. He should be here to figure this out, climb a ladder to the second story window, and remove the damn nest. I was angry with the situation and didn't want to deal with it. Thinking back now, I wonder if I missed noticing a feather or two in that debris.

I didn't know anything about animal totems back then, but since have learned a bit about their representation as spirits. Now I wonder, could that bird have been Mark keeping an eye on us? Part of me wants to be reassured by that thought and part of me is really ticked off; I hate birds and Mark knew it.

Jake thought the nest was pretty cool. I thought it was pretty gross and had no idea what to do about it. It certainly couldn't stay there. I was going to have to close the window at some point, and the overly paranoid mom in me was concerned the bird would somehow get through the screen and fly into the house. My imagination went immediately to worst-case scenarios: lice, bird poop on my bed, and terrorized children. Thank God, Mike was just downstairs. After conveying the situation to him, he took care of the unwanted visitor while I closed and locked all the windows in the house.

I can't begin to count all the ways the troops lightened my load, particularly during that first week. These seemingly small acts got me through the darkest days and carried me into the weeks ahead.

CHAPTER 7
SCHOOL

"There are no perfect moms." – Patty Slupecki

Both of our children attended a small private school that served children from preschool through eighth grade. Ellie had just started fifth grade and Jake was in the four-year-old preschool program. There were only about 300 students attending the school. This school was a special place, an extended family where everyone really did know your name. No matter who you were or what quirks you may have had, this community embraced you, cared about your kids, and came together for anyone in need.

The school nurse, Beth, who had been the first person on the accident scene when Mark was hit by a pickup truck, relayed the tragic news to the school community. Within hours plans were in motion to assist my family. Teachers and parents delivered food, the kids' friends called and visited, and the community showed their concern.

My sister, Sue, taking care of all the school related details, was in close contact with the school administrators and my kids' teachers. After keeping the kids home for a couple days, I was encouraged to send them back to school. Sue explained the routine would give them some sense of normalcy. I knew she was right, but I was scared to death to let them out of my sight. My fear was irrational, but I just couldn't bear anything happening to either of them.

I agreed to let Sue take the kids to school the next day. She had a daughter in preschool also, so she knew the people and school routine. I was comfortable with this arrangement. Sue and my mom continued taking turns transporting the kids to and from school in the beginning. After Mark's funeral, I took over the responsibility myself.

In the following months, some parents offered to drive Ellie back and forth to her after-school activities and volleyball practices. Others invited Jake to playdates and even picked him up and delivered him safely back home to me. I wasn't completely comfortable letting the kids do these things, but I knew I couldn't shield them from life. I had to let them do normal kid things. They needed to know that their life would continue, even without their Dad.

My rule about never sending anyone else to pick up my kids without telling them first had to be revised. That rule, along with many others, went to hell the day Mark died, so I improvised and created a new pickup rule with broader parameters. It included a list of family and friends, people that could potentially appear to pick them up, and the 'safe' people at school that could be trusted. In the early days, I didn't always have my act together to go get the kids at the end of the school day. My grief was debilitating and there were days I just couldn't move. Thankfully, I had this expanded tribe to rely on for getting my children home safely.

A couple weeks after the accident, I had planned to pick up the kids from school but had fallen asleep on the couch. Napping was completely out of the norm for me, but I wasn't sleeping much at night. The nap was necessary and appreciated, but somehow I missed the pickup time at school. My kids were reassured that I must be running late, and they were sent to the after-school program until I could get there. I learned later that the school called me, but I didn't answer. So, they called my mom. My mom tried calling me, but again I did not answer. It pains me to share this; my mom feared I had taken my own life. Not knowing what to do, she called my uncle to share her concern. They decided that my mom would pick up the kids and take them home with her and Uncle would drive to my house to check on me.

About an hour and a half after I had laid down on the couch, I was abruptly awakened by the ringing of my phone. I must have been in a deep sleep to not have heard the previous calls. It was my sister-in-law on the other end of the line calling to check in. I was groggy and disoriented for a moment. I asked what time it was and then flipped out when I realized I was late picking up my kids from school. Major mom-fail moment; I felt horrible! How could I have done this?

I hung up the phone and raced to the school, no doubt breaking a few speed limits along the way. I pulled up right in front of the building, into the no-parking zone, and jumped out of the car. I'm not sure I thought to turn the car off. I ran into the building, breathless, heart racing. When I made my way past the double set of entry doors, I saw my mom walking toward me with both of my children in tow. For a split second, we looked at one another puzzled by seeing the other.

I'm certain my mom was relieved to see me, but she did not share her fear with me at the time. I felt bad for inconveniencing her and the people at school. Mostly, I was sorry for scaring my kids and reassured them that I would never let this happen again. It was a promise I moved heaven and earth to keep, and I was never late again.

CHAPTER 8
THE FUNERAL HOME

"It's okay to be mad at God. It's okay to question Him. It's okay to yell and place blame. In time, a new level of faith will be understood." – Patty Slupecki

There was a queasiness in my stomach as I pushed hangers of clothing from one end of the closet to the other and back again. I was looking but not really seeing my clothes as I pushed them by. It was the day before the visitation, and my cousin, Janette, was helping me pick out something to wear to both the funeral home and funeral. Janette, who was also widowed at a very young age, had come into town to be with me through the funeral. I looked to her to tell me what to do over the course of the next two days. She had already survived burying her husband, raising their infant alone, and building her life as a strong, independent woman. In my eyes she was clearly the only person who could really understand what I was going through and guide me through this undesirable journey.

"It doesn't matter what you wear, just don't pick your favorite outfit. Whatever you choose, you'll never want to wear again," Janette advised. I understood this to be an unwritten rule, so I pushed aside the black sheath dress that I had worn out to dinner on our last wedding anniversary. Also passed over: the long, brown, sleeveless dress that tied at the waist. I wore that one on an anniversary trip to Jamaica. After I decided against a dozen or so potential choices because of the memories they triggered, I landed on a pair of black trousers and a dark blue wrap-around blouse. There were no memories attached to either of these wardrobe pieces, and the tags were still hanging from both items. They were dark, dressy, and seemed appropriate for a widow. 'Wow, a widow. I'm a widow. Is this how I will now be labeled?' It was the first time this designation came to mind, and I didn't like it.

The thought stopped me in my tracks. "Aren't widows supposed to be old, wrinkled people who had lived a long, married life?" I asked Janette as I collapsed on my bed next to her. She knew it wasn't a question that required an answer. After a few minutes of silently staring at the ceiling fan rotating slowly above me, another question gnawed at me. "Do you think Sam is in heaven?" Janette matter-of-factly responded with her thoughts on her deceased husband: "I don't believe in that. I think his body is just buried in the ground. He's just gone."

Our conversation continued about God, faith, and death. Janette had a very scientific, practical view of reality, and I was searching for what to believe and asking the universe, 'Why? Why did Mark die? Why did this happen to me? Why did this happen to my kids?' I considered myself a faithful person but not religious. Mark's death made me question that faith and God. I wondered, 'If God is real, why would He allow Mark to be killed and leave me and our kids alone? Why didn't He intervene?' The idea of not having faith in a higher power, God, made me feel sad and even more alone. In that moment, lying on the bed, I told myself, 'I won't stop believing.' If I didn't believe in God, where could I place my anger? It was all so confusing, a tornado of reasoning and questioning thoughts swirling in my head. I had to have faith that Mark's soul was still out there somewhere and that he would be watching over us. I had to hold on to this in order to move forward, to be okay, to live. I struggled with all of this and changed my mind many times, never finding any peace. Eventually, the inner turmoil surrounding my faith turned to anger. I was angry at God for not saving Mark. I wondered what I did to deserve losing my husband.

I tried on the memory-neutral outfit, and it fit. Done. I didn't care how I looked; it was simply a necessary task I needed to check off my list. I don't remember who helped with funeral clothes for Jake and Ellie; this task, like so many others, was simply handled. The three of us had clean, wrinkle-free clothes to wear to the funeral home the next day.

I was anxious about taking the kids to the visitation. The last time they saw their Dad was the morning he was hit and killed by the man in the pickup truck. I didn't know what to expect or how to prepare my children for seeing their Dad's lifeless body in a casket. I was unsure of what to say or do to make the situation less frightening and traumatic for my young children. It was like watching your child wobble at the top of a staircase from across the room. Fear starts to build. You see a fall coming, know it's going to hurt them, but can't do anything to prevent it.

The circle of family and friends around me agreed it was an important step in the grief journey for the kids to see Mark and say goodbye, so that's what I was making possible. Even though his body was going to be cremated and the casket would be closed during visitation, the funeral home prepared the body so Jake and Ellie could see their Dad one last time. He was dressed in his navy-blue suit, white shirt, favorite tie that depicted a group of runners, and signature Mickey Mouse dress socks. Mark was always teased about how many different pairs of socks he had with varying patterns of mouse ears, but the kids loved this. I'm pretty sure he wore them more for the kids than himself.

My immediate family and a few close friends were waiting for me when I arrived at the funeral home with Jake and Ellie. We were greeted with reassuring hugs and warm smiles letting me know that my children and I would be well supported on this difficult day. My tribe of advocates and champions gathered around us in a long, narrow hallway next to a series of closed double doors. The uncomfortableness of the environment was highlighted by the institutional-looking wallpaper that hung from the chair rail to the carpet lined floor. I was jolted into the reality of my situation as a well-dressed man with a name tag broke into our conversation. "The body is prepared for your private viewing. When you are ready to receive visitors, we will close the casket and then open the doors." The funeral director suggested that I take the kids in first, just the three of us. My heart was pounding in my chest, and I could feel the rhythmic pulsing in my ears. I was afraid to go in there alone, but the director was ushering me along toward one of the closed doors. I turned to Janette, "Will you come in with me?" I knew she would be strong and hold it together. Anyone else would be too emotional, and I was worried about falling apart in front of the kids. It was my job to set my feelings aside and focus on the needs of my children. I had to be strong for them, show them how tough I was, be in control, and act with confidence. At least that's how I thought I was expected to act. I don't know why I believed that; no one told me I had to be all those things. I certainly didn't feel like I was any of those things nor was I functioning normally or with much of a conscious thought process. I was merely trying to survive the moment. Maybe it was a case of mom autopilot - put yourself aside; do what has to be done.

When the door opened, I didn't have time to think about or plan my actions or words. I had to be ahead of my children to soften the blow they were about to be hit with. I walked in first with Ellie and Jake just a half a step back as though they were hiding behind me. Janette followed and then stepped aside once the door closed behind us. I remember looking back when I heard the 'clap' of solid wood doors closing. The group of familiar faces had disappeared, and I was left looking into the eyes of my two young children. "It's okay," I said out loud, really trying to convince myself more than my children. I took a deep breath as I turned to face the room again. Off to the left, I saw the casket with the lid open. The window curtains were drawn, and the room was dimly lit even though it was a bright, sunny day. I didn't like that. I hate the darkness. Straight ahead of me were rows of chairs lined up and beyond those was a large picture board. It was filled with memories in the form of photos of Mark, the kids, family, friends, and me. I couldn't make out any particular picture in the distance. As we stood there silent, motionless, I glanced further around the room, noticing how full the large room already was. Flowers, plants, and other memorial gifts filled every open space. A video was playing in two locations showcasing Mark's life in a photo montage set to music. The scrapbooks of our perfect family of four were displayed on a table beyond the casket.

I looked to Janette, waiting, hoping to be told what to do. She was across the room studying the photo board, surely keeping herself busy in this moment that belonged to Mark's wife, daughter, and son. I took another deep breath and put one arm around each child. "Let's go say goodbye to Daddy." As we approached the casket, Jake held back, his feet firmly planted on the ugly green carpeting. Ellie kept moving forward, tears in her eyes. In that split second I was torn. Do I stop to stay with one child or keep moving with the other child? Jake, having dropped the grip he had on my hand, seemed content where he was, so I stepped up next to Ellie. In a few short steps we were standing next to Mark. He looked like the man I loved, the father of our children, except he was lifeless. His smile and blue eyes were gone. The gash on his forehead that I saw covered with gauze in the ER couldn't be seen through the makeup or whatever it is that the funeral home uses to paint the face of a dead body. I looked closely and wondered for a fleeting second how it could have been made invisible.

Ellie's tears were overflowing and running down her face as she stared, wide-eyed, at her Daddy. I was helpless. I had no words, just a broken heart as I watched my little girl mourn her hero. Over my shoulder I could see Jake walking up and down the aisles between the chairs. He approached me cautiously as I stepped away from the coffin to meet him. He wasn't tall enough to see into the coffin on his own, so I scooped him up in my arms and, holding him tightly, I walked toward his Daddy's body.

"That's not Daddy." Jake was squirming in my arms, trying to break free from my grip. I gave in and released him from my protective arms. My eyes followed him as he made his way to the back corner where photos of his Dad were slowly changing on a TV screen. I decided I had to let him do what made him comfortable.

Ellie wasn't budging from the coffin. The child who never stops talking was silent. "Let's look at the flowers," I suggested, trying to break her trance. We wandered around the edges of the room stopping to look at a few cards, some planters, and lots of flowers. We passed a few memorial blanket displays and landed in front of the large photo board. Jake soon joined us as we chatted about the pictures and shared our memories of each snapshot representing a memory frozen in time. Periodically, I would glance over to Janette. I'm not sure what I expected of her, but it was reassuring to know she was there.

The funeral director returned to the room. "Would you like to invite the rest of the family in now?" I agreed. I had no sense of time or any idea how long we had been separated. The set of double doors opened, and my circle of supporters was led into the room. Silence was replaced with friendly chatter. One at a time, parents, brothers, sisters, cousins, aunts and uncles said their goodbyes to Mark. Everyone seemed pleased with how he looked; it was the hot topic of conversation in this horrible place. I didn't think dead looked good.

More visitors would be arriving soon, and it was time for the casket to be closed. The funeral home staff asked everyone to step out. "Can I stay?" I wanted to see the lid close. I wanted to know for sure that Mark's body was still there. In some odd way, it was comforting to me. My muscles were tense, and my body was heavy as I watched his body gradually sink further into the wooden box, and the lid lowered to conceal what was left of my husband. Before I felt myself take another breath all the doors were opened and a mob descended.

CHAPTER 9
A LINE OF A THOUSAND PEOPLE

*"It's okay if you don't know what to say or what to do at a visitation or funeral;
just be there. Your presence means more than you will ever know."*
— Patty Slupecki

I stood in the same place for the entire evening. It wasn't planned; it was an accident of circumstance. I had walked to the back of the room, opposite the casket, when the doors were opened for visitors, and that's where I stayed. Suddenly, people were approaching me en masse from several directions at once. It was a little disconcerting. I was unexpectedly the center of attention, which made me uncomfortable. But, it was my cross to bear, and I followed the protocol expected of a widow.

As the visitors grew in number, they seemed to politely organize themselves into a formal line that meandered around the edges of the room. There was a rumble of quiet chatter, small groups gathered around in friendly pods, and lots of eyes were fixed on me. I was grateful that so many people were taking time out of their lives to pay respects to Mark and to me. I understand now just how important it is to the grieving to simply have the physical presence of caring people.

My mom had been willingly charged with keeping track of my children while we were at the funeral home. Others stepped in to help out too. Ellie was kept occupied by the regular intervals of friends coming and going. The friends' parents had worked out a schedule ahead of time to ensure Ellie would never be alone during the visitation. Jake had some other young relatives around to play with, and when they became tired and restless, a cousin took them all home. It was such a relief to relinquish that responsibility and know my children were well cared for. All of my energy was needed for getting through the evening, and I certainly did not want to offend any well-wishers by cutting a conversation short or turning my attention elsewhere.

I'd like to tell you that I remember everyone that talked to me that night, but most of the evening is lost to me. This is why the guest-book is so critical for the bereaved. It really is the only way for me to know who was there, and I have referred to it through the years, including while writing this book. I believe it was that line of a thousand people that got me through one of the most difficult days of my life. Their presence kept me busy and focused on the constantly changing faces in front of me. I didn't have time for my thoughts to spiral out of control or think of the what-ifs.

I recognized many faces, but what really surprised me was the number of people I did not know. A few stick out in my mind because I know how much they went out of their way to be there for me. I can't express how much this meant to me and means to me still. A short woman introduced herself as someone who was at the accident site. The look on my face must have revealed my emotion because she began to apologize for not thinking to call me from the accident while Mark was still conscious. There was no need for an apology, but I think maybe this woman needed some closure for herself. We spoke only briefly, cognizant of the others waiting. I was touched by her attendance and asked her to leave her name and contact information in the guest-book so we could talk more at a later date. While I had every intention of contacting her, that day never came. My state of existence just didn't allow me to pick up the phone.

A few other people I remember included a co-worker and my boss from the pharmaceutical company I worked for at the time. The co-worker arrived with two large shopping bags filled with thoughtfully chosen gifts to help entertain my kids at the funeral home. That was a great idea and one I've copied over the years. My boss lived in Chicago and drove nearly five hours to pay his respects and then turned around and drove back home that same night. This amazed me because I really only communicated with this man on a weekly group conference call. It was another lesson in humanity; people really are good.

I was shaking a lot of hands, receiving many hugs, talking nonstop, and periodically shedding a few tears. Uncle was looking out for me. He brought me a bottle of water and even traded out my used tissues for fresh ones. I'm not sure I would have done that for someone. My father had passed away several years earlier, so I think Uncle was stepping into that role for me.

Glancing around the room at one point in the evening, my eyes followed the line of people around the large gathering space, through the open doorway, and down the hall. I couldn't see the end. I was tired of standing and wondered what the kids were doing, but held my stance and continued on with my duties as the young widow. It probably shouldn't have surprised me how many people were stopping in. Mark was one of those rare people who was liked by everyone. He was intelligent, funny, had a great work ethic, was kind to everyone, and he was the first person to jump in to help another in need. You would be hard pressed to find anyone with less than a favorable opinion of Mark.

Another memorable experience for me was the constant stream of Mark's co-workers arriving throughout the evening from several states. These people seemed to be really shaken by Mark's death, and their actions went far beyond anyone's expectations. They reached out to support us on a number of occasions during the entire first year without Mark. Donations were made periodically to the kids' educational fund, identified only as 'Mark's friends from work'. On each of the kids' first birthdays without their Dad, a bouquet of balloons was delivered along with a big jar full of candy. Again, the card was signed 'from your Dad's friends at work'. I'm still awed by the unconditional show of thoughtfulness. A number of people gave their treasure anonymously to bring a little happiness to our lives on some very difficult days.

As I write this, I find it interesting what sticks with me: the selfless giving that came from the hearts of so many people. This was incredible to me, maybe because I had a somewhat cynical, untrusting view of the human race. It's a well-learned lesson that has certainly changed my view of people and my ability to give to others without expectations. Today I choose to look for the good and trust in my positive outlook.

When we returned home that evening, Sharie went immediately in to Mark's office and created a spreadsheet documenting all of the visitors and donations made to the kids' educational fund. The fund had been set up earlier in the week in memory of Mark. I changed out of my clothes and put the tainted outfit in the back of my closet. Janette was right; I never wore that outfit again. Later that night, after the kids were asleep, Mike, Sharie and I sat down in the family room. Sharie reported there had been more than a thousand people in attendance. The three of us questioned if we even knew a thousand people collectively and shared some stories from the day. As we sat there, the light over the kitchen sink went out. It was symbolic of how I was feeling; my light had been extinguished with Mark's death. Our conversation stopped for a moment; we looked at one another and then continued. A few minutes later, the light came back on and I shook my head, wondering why I was going to have to deal with a wiring issue now of all times. The on and off pattern repeated a couple more times as if someone were trying to send us an SOS. We became fixated on the light, not moving from our seats. Finally, Mike said, "Okay Mark, we're paying attention." That was just the beginning of lights mysteriously turning on and off.

Since that time, I've read that spirits often try to get our attention by interrupting electrical current. I believe it! To this day, even in a new home, lights will sometimes go on and off for no apparent reason. It seems to only happen when I am talking or thinking about Mark. I stop momentarily, smile, and just accept it. Then I remind any spirits that may be around that I do NOT like to be scared and to NEVER do this to me in the dark of night.

CHAPTER 10
FUNERAL DAY SIGNS

"Signs are all around us, if we choose to see them." – Patty Slupecki

J ake was sick and throwing up, and my stomach was in knots as I sat on the couch holding my little boy. I kept repeating to myself, 'not today, please God not today.' The house was already abuzz with activity and people preparing to leave for the funeral. Sue arrived with a baked potato and proceeded to butter it, mash it, and load up a fork with a bite for me. She thought I might be able to eat something a little bland to calm my nerves and nourish my weakening body. I hadn't eaten for the last week and the lack of food was beginning to take a toll on my already fragile existence. That first bite was like trying to swallow while my neck was being squeezed. There was a blockage that I just couldn't get through. I simply could not make myself eat. Sipping some water was the most I could tolerate; it would have to do for now.

I tried to cajole Jake into getting dressed for the funeral, but he laid limp on my lap. I offered every bribe I could conceive: candy, toys, staying up late. Nothing would entice him. 'Okay,' I thought, 'I'll just take him to the funeral in his pajamas. Who cares? He's a little 4-year-old boy going to his father's funeral.' And then he threw up again.

My mom and sister suggested that maybe this day was simply too much for Jake to deal with and he might be better off staying home. I struggled with this idea and wondered if, down the road, he would be upset with me for not insisting he attend the funeral. I didn't know what to do. I didn't want to make the wrong decision. Who would stay with him if I left him behind? What would Mark want?

After agonizing over the decision, my mom and Sue suggested we try to find someone to stay with Jake. I agreed and made a few suggestions, but this proved more difficult than any of us anticipated. The people I called wanted to be at the funeral. I understood their reasons, but it was a blow that knocked me off balance. In the end, it was my long-time housekeeper that stepped in to care for Jake while the rest of us attended the funeral. She had planned to clean the house while we were gone so it would look presentable for visitors after the funeral luncheon. I didn't care anymore what my house looked like; I was only concerned that Jake be cared for while I was gone. Later that day I found out that as soon as everyone left the house, Jake got up off the couch and started playing. That poor little boy just needed some quiet and calmness in his environment.

Once we arrived at the church, Ellie and I sat in the first pew. I was having a Mass because I knew it would be important to Mark. He was always the one to encourage our regular attendance and raise our children in the church we both grew up in. While I'm a faithful person and consider myself spiritual, I was never a fan of organized religion. Ever the lover of riling me up, Mark would take a large bill from his wallet to put into the weekly collection basket. I would react with complete horror that he would drop so much cash, anonymously, into the deep pockets of the Catholic Church. Sometimes I warned him that if he put too much in, I would take change back out when the basket passed me. Of course, I never did; I was just trying to get even with Mark for rattling my cage. He would get the biggest grin on his face when he knew he got to me. I miss that.

Mark's body was to be cremated, so I guess the funeral home assumed there was no need to bring the casket to the church. It never crossed my mind until I was sitting there that Mark's body should have been at the service. Damn! It was too late to do anything about it. Why hadn't the funeral director asked me? After all, they did charge me $1,000 to rent the damn casket, which still pisses me off! Maybe he did ask, and I just don't remember. I was going along with whatever anyone said or told me to do during the planning process. Some people had very strong opinions as to what they wanted. I didn't care; it didn't matter. My husband was dead. I just nodded in agreement to stop the talking and questioning.

After the funeral and following luncheon in the church hall, many people returned to my home. It was time to change clothes, pour some drinks, and let the kids outside to run around. Everyone around me seemed relieved and more relaxed. The hard part for them was over. They could return to their normal lives and be distracted by their regular routines. For me, the hard part was just beginning.

After arriving back home, I overheard a conversation about the accident site. Apparently, several close family members and friends had gone to see the place where Mark was hit. Why didn't I know about this? Why didn't anyone tell me? Why didn't they take me? I pulled Mike aside and questioned him. He assured me that no one was keeping anything from me; they were only trying to spare me more pain. I asked Mike to take me there, right then, and he willingly agreed.

The two of us drove out to the country road and parked alongside the cornfield. We got out of the car and walked around the area. I identified some green plastic pieces in the rough edge of the road that had once been Mark's water bottle. Mike explained to me what he knew and how authorities think the accident happened. He showed me the ditch where Mark was lying after smashing into the windshield of the pickup truck. We stopped there, quiet for a moment, and I looked down. In the flattened-out area of high weeds where rescuers had worked to stabilize Mark's broken, bleeding body, was a soft, gently curved, white feather. I gasped and pointed it out to Mike. It was *my* first feather, and in that moment I felt a sense of closure.

I told Mike, "This is my book." I instantly knew that I needed to write about feathers from heaven as a way to comfort the grieving. My intention was, and still is, to write a children's book using this story. I've started it and worked on it periodically over the years, but I'm not yet ready to share it.

When we arrived back home, the funeral home was delivering all of the flower arrangements, plants, and gifts that had been displayed at the visitation the day before. There were so many, I didn't know what to do with them. The house was full of people, so I told the driver to just leave them in the front yard. Mike and I stood there as the van was unloaded.

When the driver finished, he explained that he had some papers for me to sign. Mike took over the conversation for me as the funeral home representative gave a disclaimer speech. He rattled on about cremation, explaining graphic details about bone fragments and the mix of ashes from previous cremations. I thought I would faint, but Mike stepped slightly forward, leaving me physically and emotionally protected by his shoulder. Shaken too, Mike interrupted the idiot spewing the harsh words and told me to just sign the paper and go inside. The anger is resurfacing in me as I write this. I can feel my face flushing and my jaw tightening. How could that man have been so insensitive? No more words will be wasted on this man.

Back inside, I could hear cheerful talking and laughter coming from the dining room. I walked robotically toward the sounds and silently entered the group gathered around the table. I stood there pretending to be engaged with the conversation and forcing a smile when anyone made eye contact with me. I wanted everyone to leave, but I didn't want to be alone. One of the kids came running in from the backyard, breaking my thoughts. He was telling our group of adults to come see the rainbow. It was a perfectly clear day. The sun was shining and there wasn't a cloud in the sky, but he persisted until my mother-in-law decided to investigate. Soon, she was hollering for us all to come outside. We conceded and made our way out to the back deck where we all looked into the sky in the direction of her pointed finger. There was silence as we witnessed a bright semicircle of a rainbow turned upside down in the blue sky. We stared at it for what seemed like several minutes and agreed that none of us had ever seen anything like it before. My mother-in-law sent one of the kids in for her camera; there were no cell phone cameras then. But by the time she was in possession of her camera and poised for the shot, the rainbow had faded away.

As you know by now, I totally believe in signs from heaven and those who have passed. I believe in spirit guides and the ability to communicate with the other side. Isn't faith believing in the existence of things you can't necessarily see or touch? I've learned to stop looking for proof and just accept this faith, my faith. It brings me peace. I'm sure Mark sent that smiling rainbow to us. I learned a few days later that the only times upside-down rainbows had been seen or at least recorded was following a death. I don't need any further explanation. My heart is content with the belief I have. But that wasn't the only sign delivered to us that day.

A little later that day, in the early evening, some of the kids went back outside only to return moments later reporting another unusual sight. Somewhat reluctantly, I went outside to discover the lawn covered in white baby bird feathers. Well, if the smiling rainbow didn't have you questioning messages from the spirit world, then surely a yard full of feathers has rocked your stance on the subject.

A smile crossed my face. The kids were scooping up the feathers and tossing them into the air, much like they would a pile of leaves in the fall. As others filled the deck once again, there was a quiet sense of awe and wonder among the believers. Words seemed to fail most of us witnessing this truly remarkable experience. One of the adults broke the silence with a joke about a bird fight, but I didn't acknowledge it. I held firm to my belief that those perfect little feathers were delivered straight from Heaven. For a few moments, I could breathe a little easier. I knew Mark was okay and that he would be watching over us. The small sense of relief was a much-welcomed diversion from the pain of the past week not only for me but for everyone open to receiving.

CHAPTER 11
FRIENDS ARE GREAT…
AND THEN THEY LEAVE

"Give freely of yourself, your time, and your resources to those in need without the expectation of acknowledgment." – Patty Slupecki

People rally around when a tragedy hits their community. We see that with natural disasters like hurricanes, flooding, and tornadoes. We see it when a terrorist attacks or in the aftermath of a school shooting. We see it with serious injuries, terminal illness, and sudden, unexpected death.

I was a skeptic when it came to trusting others, their intentions, actions, or words. It's sad when I think back on this now, but I learned a valuable lesson about people: Most people really are good, kind, and well-intentioned. Being the recipient of so many thoughtful actions truly amazed me and left a significant imprint on my heart. For the first time in my life, I experienced and recognized true gratefulness. It forever changed the way I view the world.

After Mark died, I was blessed with overwhelming kindness

from family, friends, acquaintances, and even from people I did not know. As I later learned, I wasn't even aware of some of the people or actions, yet people did nice things anyway, without recognition or thanks.

It's been nearly 16 years as I write this, and I still feel badly about missing thank-you notes and often wonder what else I may be unaware of today. I want the thanked and unthanked people to know how much I appreciated every kindness. I want them to know that I continue to pay it forward in honor of them.

My memory of those first couple of weeks is almost nonexistent. Certainly I was in shock, numb, and completely tuned out of life. The brain is a magnificent thing, sparing us from recalling our most traumatic moments. Over time, some memories have surfaced; stories have been relayed to me by others, and there are some that stand out to me.

One particular act of kindness occurred in the few short days between Mark's death and his funeral. Several scrapbooking friends and acquaintances gathered at a neighbor's home to assemble two large photo albums showcasing Mark's life and the story of our once happy family.

Creating elaborate scrapbooks was a popular hobby back in 2002, and I had jumped on the crafting bandwagon. It was our Facebook before the world went digital. The practice of displaying photo boards, albums, and memorabilia to remember and honor the deceased had become expected during funeral visitations. I wanted my scrapbooks filled with pictures so visitors could see and remember Mark's life.

I had stacks of presorted family photos, separated by squares of cardboard and enclosed in two-inch-thick boxes. The boxes were secured with rubber bands and were waiting on my top closet shelf to be trimmed, secured on scrapbook pages, and enhanced with stickers, borders, and backgrounds.

While I wanted to share the memories of Mark, I couldn't bring myself to shuffle through the photos. It was too soon, too painful.

The scrapbooking group collected my boxes and organized them to complete my albums. They must have spent many hours away from their own families to focus their time and talent on my family memories. I'm certain that working on this project also cost these friends some cash, which no one ever mentioned to me.

Another significant memory is of my friend, Annie. She called me as soon as she heard the news and announced that she would be arriving the week after Mark's funeral. How did she know that was just what I needed? She made all the arrangements to fly in from California and stay with me for an entire week after everyone else went home. I didn't have to think or do anything. She even rented a car, so I didn't have to pick her up at the airport an hour away from my home. I was so grateful.

I wasn't ready to be on my own or figure out how the hell to play the role of both mom and dad. Mark and I had been a team, divide and conquer. I cooked dinner, he cleaned up. I helped Ellie with homework, he gave Jake a bath. I managed the inside of the house, he kept up with the outside. It was two full-time jobs, and I didn't want to take on both. I didn't want to be left alone.

Annie was a Godsend. I didn't want life to keep moving all around me. It made me dizzy because I was stopped, stuck in time. But she pushed me through the day-to-day life events and sat right next to me for moral support. I got up and dressed each day, not for myself, but because I had no choice. I had to bring back some kind of routine for my kids' sake. I began taking them to school and picking them up again instead of my mom doing it. Annie and I went to Ellie's volleyball game and Jake's soccer game. I was gently lead through the day by Annie.

One evening toward the end of her stay, Annie said she was going out to meet some old friends. I panicked. It was like that feeling you get the very first time you hold a newborn child. There's uncertainty in your ability to do it right. It's uncomfortable and awkward. I didn't know what to do all by myself. Or maybe, I was just scared to be solely responsible for this new, unwanted life.

It was months or maybe longer before I realized how incredibly attuned Annie was to my needs. She knew I had to be on my own and purposely weaned me from having constant support at my side. Over her last couple of days with me, she spent more time out of the house during my peak panic hours. She did this without ever telling me her intention. It gave me the opportunity to stand on my own for short periods of time with the reassurance of knowing another adult would soon be back with me.

When Annie returned to her own life, job, and responsibilities, I was officially alone. Mark wasn't coming home at the end of the day to relieve me of parenting duties or engage me in adult conversation. My family and friends had returned to the demands of their own lives. Every evening that fall became darker outside and inside as I stumbled to find a new routine for my kids and myself. However, thanks to Annie, I was at least going through the motions of surviving.

Another act of incredible kindness was nearly four months of meal deliveries. Friends, neighbors, and some people I did not even know, filled in a weekly dinner delivery calendar. They kept us fed from the longer days of September through the darker nights of December. Three days a week, dinner would arrive between late afternoon and early evening.

The logistics had to be managed on paper and by phone; there were no online organization tools for providing meals like there are today. Someone had to keep track of the schedule and make phone call reminders to the volunteers. That was a lot of work!

Early in the dinner schedule, my friend, Paul, arrived at my front door wearing shorts, a baseball jersey, and his signature backward-facing ball cap. There were plastic grocery bags hanging from both arms, and he was holding a foil-covered pan containing his secret recipe, homemade meatballs.

I remember this well because I was having a difficult time eating, so much that I had dropped to 100 pounds, and my doctor was threatening to put me in the hospital if I didn't stop losing weight. Eating had never been a problem for me, and it certainly isn't now. I've always thoroughly enjoyed food. I knew I needed to eat to stay healthy for my kids' sake if not my own. I tried to eat, but just the sight of food would cause my throat to start closing. The once lovely aromas of freshly made foods suddenly made my stomach turn.

When Paul removed the foil cover to present his dish, I was met with the fragrance of Italian spices and fresh tomato sauce. It smelled so good that I actually wanted to eat a meatball, and I did. This was a turning point. I put the meatballs and red sauce in a plastic container and hid it in the back of the refrigerator. This was one dinner I wasn't going to share.

For the next several days, my goal was to eat one meatball each day. They were about the size of a clementine, and it would take me a half hour or so to eat it, but I was able to eat it and keep it down. After a week of eating meatballs, I was able to gradually introduce other foods back into my diet. It was still a challenge to eat, and I had to consciously make an effort to try a bite of food here and there.

Paul's meatballs weren't the only delicious comfort foods we received. Jake's preschool teachers delivered a large, cheesy pan of lasagna that oozed over the sides of the dish and a homemade apple pie that smelled like my grandmother's kitchen. There were pans of creamy macaroni and cheese, casseroles of chicken and rice, and pots of chicken noodle soup made by friends that arrived like clockwork.

Why is it, that in times of sadness and celebration, we feel the need to offer food? Not just any food either; we offer comfort foods. You know, the foods heavy in carbs, fat, and sugar. There is an entire science dedicated to the study of these foods on our brains. Those aren't the details I want to dwell on. I just think it's amazing that most people default, without much thought, to food in times of need.

Maybe the reason somehow relates to a sense of community and comfort. A hot meal fills us up figuratively and literally. I guess cooking food provides us with something to do, a way we can be helpful especially when we don't know what to do or how to help.

It was helpful not having to think about what I would feed the kids each night for dinner. The large meals complete with side dishes and desserts reminded me of family dinners, family dinners I wasn't cooking and would never have again. Without Mark, my family wasn't whole. I was now a widow with two small children, not a family.

As the weeks passed, my community returned to their own normal lives, while my life was spiraling into nothingness. There was no normal in my existence, only survival. The large tribe that surrounded me in my moment of tragedy began to dwindle. Homemade meals became pizza delivery and restaurant gift cards. I certainly don't mean to sound ungrateful; I am merely emphasizing that for everyone outside of my house, life as they knew it had returned. They went to work, socialized, played with their happy kids, and complained about their spouses and busy schedules. I did not.

Occasionally, the kids and I were invited out to eat with friends or into their homes for dinner. I always appreciated the thoughtful invitations, but it was difficult for me to go. It wasn't that I didn't want to go, but rather, I didn't want to have to return home, alone with the kids in the darkness of evening. I hated the thought of entering that big, empty house where my once happy family used to live. It was a painful reminder that Mark was gone. Just the thought of it drained the blood from my face. I was afraid to be alone in the dark, solely responsible for the safety of my children.

The nights were always the worst time for me, and they kept getting longer, darker, and colder. As time passed, the sun was setting earlier each day and rising later every morning. The universe seemed to be taking away the little comfort I had in the daylight hours, minute by minute. It felt like a slow and painful tearing of a Band-Aid from my fragile skin. I often thought to myself, 'It's not fair. Why me?'

I would sometimes push myself to accept an invitation, but the anxiety of returning home alone would make me begin to panic. I couldn't eat or focus on a conversation with the dread building inside me, eating away any last bit of self-confidence.

It was easier and far less stressful to stay home in a somewhat level amount of pain and anxiety than it was to go out and endure the spikes of emotional upheaval, so I began making excuses for not accepting invitations. Eventually, the invitations became less frequent and then stopped. They left me. I was alone again.

I'm well aware that no longer receiving invitations was my own doing, but nevertheless, not hearing the phone ring was lonely. It doesn't seem rational, I know. I didn't want to go anywhere, but I also didn't want people to stop asking. Numbness was firmly settled in. I couldn't make sense of it myself, let alone explain to others my opposing feelings and actions, nor did I have the energy to even try. I felt guilty. I wanted to thank them for their efforts, but I just couldn't bring myself to do it. It was as if my body were paralyzed, unable to perform the tasks my brain knew I should be doing.

When the phone did ring, I didn't answer because I simply couldn't make conversation. I would hope the person on the other end would leave a message to distract me from the crippling grief so I would not feel so alone for just a moment. At the same time, I hoped they didn't want me to call back because I knew I wouldn't. I couldn't. Every ounce of energy I had was spent making sure my kids were okay, and sometimes I felt I failed at that.

Every waking minute felt like I was trudging through waist-high mud, rain pelting down hard on my face, the wind blowing me backwards. It took more energy than any physical excursion I'd ever experienced, and the setbacks were many. One step forward in surviving another hour, then two steps back in half an hour. When would it get better? When would there be some relief?

I appreciated it when friends would just do things without asking, like my neighbor, Don. He worked odd hours and would oftentimes be up in the middle of the night. During the first winter without Mark, we had a fair amount of snowfall. On several occasions, I was awake in the dark hours when the kids were sleeping and would hear the faint scraping noise of a shovel being pushed along the cement. From my second floor bedroom window, I could see Don under the glow of the streetlight shoveling the snow from my driveway and sidewalk. He never rang the doorbell or called, he just did it so I didn't have to.

As I write this, it seems absurd that I had such incapacitating fear about the things I did on a regular basis. When Mark would travel for work I was alone with the kids for a few days and managed to do just fine. Ellie was old enough to work on her homework and shower on her own; I just had to tell her to do it and check on her. There was very little effort required on my part, yet now it was an overwhelming task.

When Mark was completing his MBA, he often needed time out of the house in the evening in order to study or attend class. I was perfectly capable of taking care of the kids and house on my own then. But now, the thought of doing anything alone exhausted me; it took too much energy, energy I just didn't have.

In those early days, weeks, and months, the house felt so big and empty. The kids needed so much attention and had meltdowns frequently as they dealt with losing their dad. I didn't feel capable of handling so many unwanted emotions, both from my kids and myself.

Other friends would continue to offer kindnesses periodically, like taking the kids to events or having them over to play with friends. Part of me was afraid to let my kids out of my sight; I was still fearful of something bad happening to them. On the other hand, I welcomed the break from the constant care that two small children require.

A neighbor and friend, Dorothy, would make regular stops to check on me during the day when the kids were in school. She baked the most delicious oatmeal raisin cookies and would often bring a plate with her. Those raisin-filled bites of subtle sweetness were the next thing I was able to eat after Paul's meatballs. And yes, I hid those too.

We played tennis together and Dorothy encouraged me to get back on the court just to focus on something different for a while. She was very intuitive, like Annie, knowing what I really needed and gently guiding me through the process. Dorothy began picking me up for tennis on Sunday evenings. She would call to remind me, leaving a voice mail every weekend without fail. This gave me no excuse to not show up, and it provided me with one activity just for myself. My mom would come over and stay with the kids while I was gone. It was an enormous relief knowing there was another adult waiting for me at home after tennis.

Another thing that Dorothy generously did for me was to write all of the thank-you notes after Mark's funeral. Knowing how grateful I was for every kindness shown to my family, Dorothy acknowledged all of the well-wishers at a time that I was unable to do so.

She took the lists compiled by my sister-in-law, Sharie, of those who visited the funeral home, those who made donations to Ellie and Jake's education fund, those who sent flowers and gifts, those who delivered dinners, and those who wrote notes. She took care of every aspect-- getting the thank-you note cards from the funeral home, finding addresses in my Rolodex, and stamping and mailing all the notes on my behalf. What a gift that was for me.

While the outpouring of unconditional love and kindness taught me many things, one of the most important life lessons I still carry with me today is this: Give freely of myself, my time, and my resources to those in need without the expectation of acknowledgment.

CHAPTER 12
DADDY BOXES

"Grief is a journey that each of us must walk in our own way, in our own time."
– Patty Slupecki

At 4 and 10 years old, the kids experienced and dealt with grief in very different ways although grief came out mostly in behaviors instead of words for both of them. At such young ages, they weren't equipped with the language to express themselves. At 37, I wasn't equipped to deal with this either, but I didn't have a choice. I had to figure it out in order to help my kids because it was my responsibility as their mom. I didn't have a road map, didn't know what to do, and didn't know how to help. I just stumbled my way through it...for years.

Jake didn't understand the permanence of the situation, and he had no idea how this would forever affect his life. He couldn't anticipate the future 'donuts with dads,' birthday parties, graduations, or holidays without his Dad. As a preschooler, Jake operated in the here and now. When things weren't going just so, he screamed for his Daddy. This could be brought on by a scraped knee, bath time, or exhaustion. I remember one time in particular: The toilet in the kids' bathroom overflowed and it terrified Jake. When I rushed upstairs to investigate the hysterical screaming, he was jumping up and down in the hallway outside the bathroom, insisting that only Daddy could fix it! I splashed through the puddling water on the floor and turned off the valve under the toilet to stop the flow of water filling the bathroom. I tried to assure Jake that it was okay and that I could fix it. I tried to hold him in my arms and rock him like I did when he was an infant, but he continued to cry for Daddy. You might as well have ripped my heart right out of my chest. Daddy was the one thing I couldn't give him, and nothing I could do was helping to ease his pain. I sat on the floor in the narrow hallway with Jake in my lap. I quietly cried to myself, praying to God, begging for calmness and dreading the cleanup. Jake finally settled down and fell asleep on the floor next to me. I didn't want to move. I was empty, tired, and completely swallowed in self-pity. Eventually I summoned enough energy to carry my little boy to bed and began mopping and plunging.

Ellie had six years on Jake; her level of maturity and understanding did recognize the complete change in her life caused by this sudden loss. She questioned her security and stability. She worried about having to move out of our home and leaving her school and friends. Thank God, neither was the case. Mark had planned well to provide financial security for his family.

Ellie kept her grief bottled up inside, refusing to talk about her feelings and focusing more on practicalities like money. At one point, she shut down at school, stopped doing her work, and would doodle on test papers instead of answering the questions. Everything in her life had been turned upside down, and she had no control over it. Doing or not doing schoolwork was an opportunity for her to exhibit some kind of control. While I know and completely understand this today, at the time I did not. In hindsight, I did all the wrong things to get her to do her schoolwork. I was mad that I was paying a handsome tuition for her education and she was not taking advantage of the opportunity. I grounded her, I took away television and technology, and I tried to bribe her. Nothing I tried was working, and

I was growing increasingly frustrated; she was just as bullheaded as I was. Mark had always been the voice of reason and the buffer between Ellie and me. I was mad at him for not being here to once again be our go-between.

I felt sorry for myself. I was angry not only about being an only parent left to deal with raising the kids alone but also having to deal with the emotional aftermath of a dead parent. Sometime after many unsuccessful attempts to punish Ellie, it occurred to me that I was trying to take away the only little bit of control she could exert in her life. I was also taking away the few things she enjoyed during that awful time. Another mom fail! I felt terrible discovering I was making everything worse for my grieving child. I beat myself up pretty good over my wrong choices. If only I had known then what I know now, maybe I could have spared us both some of the emotional baggage we had to drag around.

Of all the pain I suffered from losing Mark, witnessing my children's pain was the greatest. Being unable to console them was rubbing salt in my wounds. As a mom, all I wanted was to make it better, wipe the tears away, and bring a smile to their sad faces with a simple ice cream cone. Grief cannot be fixed with a sweet treat, a hug, or even reassuring sentiments. It is a journey that each of us must walk in our own way and time. It's a deeply personal process that is constantly changing. What comforts one may not comfort another. There are no rules and many opinions on what the right things to do are.

The most disheartening thing I learned about children and grief came from the grief counselor I took the kids to see. He told me that both the kids would have to go through their grieving process with every developmental stage they went through. Just when I was thinking that it couldn't get any worse, the answer punched me in the face and shoved my head in the dirt. What a blow this information was for me. How was I going to make it through years of dealing with this shit when I was only holding together by a thread?

Right after Mark's death, Jake and Ellie wanted their Dad's stuff. I could see they were both desperate to have tangible memories of him. If they couldn't hug their dad, then they needed to physically hold things that belonged to him. The kids started wearing Mark's tees as nightshirts instead of their own pajamas to bed at night. Mark had an enormous collection of tees he'd saved over the years from participating in various races. Jake and Ellie each chose their favorite shirts and moved them into their own dressers. Ellie chose based on memories she had of being with her dad for a race. Her first pick was from a race that Mark won in his age group. The winner got to kiss a pig and Ellie thought that was the funniest prize ever. Jake seemed to choose based on color or crazy design. They both had their own ideas of what represented their Dad.

I wore Mark's tees also, except for the one he was wearing the morning he was killed. He left it hanging over the treadmill in our bedroom where he had changed his clothes before he left for the bike ride. It smelled like him, and he put it there; I didn't want it moved. I wanted it exactly where and how he left it and felt that way about most of his belongings. But the kids wanted his things with them in their own rooms and I understood how important it was to them. I told the kids they could have whatever they wanted. Fortunately, neither wanted the shirt on the treadmill.

Immediately, Ellie choose a few framed pictures of Mark and an Ohio State sweatshirt. Jake wanted the gold medical ID necklace that Mark wore every day. It hung on a long gold chain and identified him as an insulin dependent diabetic. Jake also wanted Mark's watch, not his dress watch, the one he wore running to time himself and track his progress, the one he was wearing when he died.

Over time, the collections grew as the kids came across things in the house that sparked a memory or maybe just an interest. These items were precious to the kids and I wanted to keep them safe, so I purchased two under-the-bed storage containers made of heavy, clear plastic. I gave one to each of the kids and explained how the boxes would be a place to hold all their memories of their dad. We named them Daddy Boxes. The boxes would be available for quick access any time they wanted to add something or to look through the treasures.

Looking through the Daddy Boxes became a regular activity for both kids. While it was heartbreaking for me to see them sitting on their bedroom floor gently touching each item in their box, it seemed to be helpful for them. For me, it was a sucker punch to the gut. There were occasions when I would hear one of the kids crying behind a closed bedroom door. Before I even opened the door I knew what I'd find, and I dreaded going in to deal with it. There would be a grieving child, my child, surrounded by items that used to belong to Mark. There was no way to ease the pain for them; I couldn't fix it or make it better. As a mom, I was usually able to magically relieve sadness with a hug, a distraction, or a treat. But grief is a monster that I could not battle for my children, and I felt inadequate in my job as a mom. All I could do was sit with my grieving children, hold them, cry with them, and tell them we would all be okay. I said it, but I wasn't sure it was true. I didn't know how we would be okay or even what to do next on the road to okay. What would "okay" look like? I had no idea, but I assured my children we'd get there. I knew I had no choice but to figure it out for them.

At first, grief had total control over me. I wouldn't see it coming and couldn't avoid it. I would lose it, break down, cry, and plead with God to bring Mark back. Sometimes these breakdowns lasted a few minutes and other times a few hours. I had to figure out how to hold it together for the kids' sake. Then I learned a little trick from the kids' grief counselor. It was a technique for compartmentalizing my life and emotions, and it served me well for many years.

The basic premise is this: When there was something, a feeling, an emotion, frustration, a conversation, or grief that I didn't want to deal with, I would imagine putting it into a jelly jar, screwing the lid on tight, and placing it on a shelf to deal with at a later date. In my mind's eye, I built several very long wooden shelves and filled them with quart jars instead of jelly jars. Using this visualization trick helped me survive those first few years and stay focused on my kids' grief journey and needs instead of my own, most of the time. Eventually, I learned this practice was one of the things keeping me stuck in the victim role, preventing me from moving forward.

Today, Jake and Ellie still have their Daddy Boxes and I have one too. The boxes are filled, sealed, and tucked away for safekeeping. There is a comfort in knowing these tangible memories exist should we ever want to revisit them.

CHAPTER 13
THE BOOK STORE TRIP

"There are no coincidences. Every dot along our journey connects to the next."
– Patty Slupecki

During those early weeks, my sister would come over to my house every day after the kids were off to school. She was an enormous help dealing with the mail, paying the bills, and generally taking care of the details of my life. I was still completely numb, unable to function on my own, only able to follow simple directives of the friends and family who swooped in to take care of Ellie, Jake, and me. Unable to get through the day alone, I did exactly what I was told and was grateful for those who stepped in to navigate the world for me.

On one particular morning, Sue was in the small room just off the front door that I used as my home office. There were files and mail stacked high in several piles across my black, L-shaped desk. Sue was digging through the paperwork aftermath that follows the death of a person. Every account and asset needed to be transferred from joint ownership with Mark to my name alone.

Alone, there's that word again. I hated that word for a very long time.

The paperwork was a nightmare that required sending out roughly three dozen death certificates to prove my husband was dead. Can you believe it? Nothing like rubbing salt in a very raw wound! It eventually took a full two years to complete all of the required forms so that I could be the lone owner of our home, cars, investments, and bank accounts. However, the need for Mark's death certificate continues to this day.

I heard the phone ringing in the office, but I didn't move. Sue answered it and I could hear her side of the conversation. "Okay, she'll be ready."

A feeling of dread came over me. What was I going to have to do now?

Sue came into the living room where I was sitting on the couch, staring into the center of the room. There was no television or radio on; I didn't have a book or magazine. I was just staring into nothingness.

My friend, Trish, had called. Sue announced to me that Trish was going to the bookstore and stated that I was going with her. "She will be here in five minutes to pick you up."

I didn't want to go to the bookstore, but I had no energy to argue. Looking back, I'm so grateful that Sue kept me moving forward. By insisting that I participate in the mundane events of life like going shopping with a friend or to the pumpkin patch with the kids, Sue kept me alive - or at least pretending to be living. She helped me keep some semblance of normalcy for Jake and Ellie's sake.

Sue opened the heavy, brown front door to watch for Trish through the glass storm door. The living room was off the front hallway, opposite the office. That's where I continued sitting, motionless, empty, and overcome with the feeling of being completely lost. I didn't have to 'get ready.' What was there to 'get ready'? I didn't care about what I was wearing or how my hair or makeup looked. I didn't recognize being warm or cold. I didn't really know if I had two shoes on my feet. Those things didn't even cross my mind; they didn't matter.

My attention turned to the front door when Trish came in. Together, Sue and Trish prodded me up off the couch and out the door. 'Fine.' I thought. 'I'll go along just to make them happy.'

Trish drove us to the big box bookstore over by the mall. We got out of the car and walked to the entrance. I fell several steps behind as if I were a child being dragged somewhere I didn't want to go. Once we finally entered the bookstore, Trish said, "I have to go ask about this book. You can come with me or go wander around for a few minutes."

Again, as if I were a child, I was given two simple choices. I'm not complaining; I needed this direction at the time.

I decided to wander around.

I wasn't looking for anything in particular, just scanning the shelves as I passed. Nothing came into focus for me; I saw books but not titles. I saw shelves but not genres. I was just putting one foot in front of the other to stay upright until I could go back home.

I rounded the corner of a long aisle and there, at the very end, on the bottom shelf, sat a small book, face out, with a blue and beige cover. I'm not sure why it caught my attention. I did notice the soothing colors, small size, and the fact it was hardbound. I couldn't read the title, nor did I try. I also couldn't muster the energy to bend all the way over to reach it on the bottom shelf, so I moved along.

That little book stayed in my head, drawing me in. Curiosity got the best of me, and I turned around and went back to locate the book again. This moment was one of the first sparks of life returning to me. I was interested in something and pursued it. When I reached the corner shelf again, I stood there looking at the book trying to decide if I could bend down to reach it. I finally did, and when I stood back up I read the title for the first time: *When God Winks* by Squire Rushnell. I thought that seemed interesting and thumbed through the short book, stopping to rest on a random page.

I looked at a line midway down the page and read, "You did not pick up this book by coincidence." My eyes grew wide, my curiosity spiked, and I knew I had to have this book. As I learned in the days following my discovery, the author offers the idea that coincidences are really signposts that help us navigate the various aspects of our lives. The trick is in being open-minded enough to see them.

It was just about that time when Trish came down the aisle looking for me. "You found something! That's great. Do you want to keep looking?" she asked. "No," I replied, holding my treasure close. "I'm ready to go."

We entered the short checkout line, and I was immediately called to cashier # 2. The young woman behind the computer placed my purchase into an oversized, white plastic bag with some advertising on one side. I was actually looking forward to reading my new book and anxious to get home so I could begin.

Though not a religious person, I am a spiritual person. I believe in a higher power, spirit guides, and signs from the other side. It is beyond my comprehension how I would have survived this great tragedy without my faith. But my faith was shaken; I questioned why God would let my husband die. I stopped attending church, and I struggled to hold onto my faith. I was mad at God.

Squire Rushnell defines a God Wink as, "A personal signal or message, directly from a higher power, usually, but not always, in the form of a coincidence." Finding *When God Winks* was a turning point for me. My anger and questions didn't disappear, but they did start to consume less of my energy and time. I began to search for peace rather than answers.

When Trish dropped me back off at home, Sue was still in my office. She said she was researching some books on death and dying that might be helpful for Ellie and Jake. She continued to explain that *Charlotte's Web* was highly recommended for children dealing with loss and grief and went into a few details.

After Sue finished reporting her finds, she asked, "Did you buy something?" pointing to the bag in my hand. "Oh yes," I replied with a glimmer of excitement in my voice. I began sharing the story of how I found the little book. As I talked, I placed the bag down on the desk in front of Sue and suddenly stopped mid-sentence, uttering an audible gasp. "What's wrong?" Sue quickly asked. "Look!" I directed, pointing at the bookstore bag.

The writing on the outside of the bookstore bag was an advertisement for *Charlotte's Web*. "There are no coincidences," I said. This was the beginning of a new and wonderful faith journey for me.

CHAPTER 14
WHERE AM I?

"There is nothing more amazing or powerful than learning to control your thoughts. When you control your thoughts, you control your life."
— Patty Slupecki

I hadn't driven my car much in the weeks following the funeral, and the first time I gathered the courage to leave the house alone was a milestone for me. It took a lot of energy to propel myself forward. I was frightened to be out in the world without the security of someone by my side. I know it sounds silly, but I wasn't yet finding my way into a new normal. Eventually, with my sister's encouragement, I pushed myself to run a few errands. It felt odd to be back in my car again; I had to give the dashboard a quick once over to reacquaint myself with the dials and buttons. I took a deep breath, reassured myself that I could do this, and bravely proceeded out to accomplish my necessary errands.

All of a sudden, as if I had just woken up from a deep sleep, I was lost, confused about where I was or how I even got there. I found myself behind the wheel of my Jeep, in the left turn lane, stopped at a traffic light. I remember shaking my head as if trying to clear the fog and regain my wits. I had no recollection of where I intended to go. A bit of panic rose in my stomach, and when the light changed, I made the turn and pulled into a parking lot. My breathing was fast and heavy, like I had just finished a workout. Looking around, I recognized my surroundings and that gave me momentary relief.

I consciously left my house with the intention of running errands. I remembered that much, but from the time I turned out of my neighborhood until that moment of sudden awareness, my memory was a complete blank. I couldn't remember why I was in the car. I couldn't remember driving that four miles away from home. Where was I going? What if I had gotten into an accident? What do I do now? There was a rush of what-ifs running through my mind.

I sat still in the car for a few minutes and waited for the panic to subside. Remembering I had written down the errands I planned to run, I searched my purse and found the yellow sticky note. Thank God I was, and still am, a list maker. I was relieved to know where I was and where I was going but having no memory of driving was really concerning me. When I felt alert enough to continue, I placed the sticky note in the center of the steering wheel and pressed it down several times ensuring it would remain in place. I took great care in paying attention to the road and referred to my note often.

For nearly that whole first year after Mark was killed, I needed to write out where I intended to go and what I needed to do. Large yellow sticky notes became my copilot every time I left the house. I continued to find myself suddenly aware of my surroundings without realizing how I got there. It always gave me a jolt of adrenalin, but I had conquered the fear. The visual reminder on my steering wheel would quickly place me back in reality although sometimes a few miles out of the way. I relied heavily on that list to accomplish even the simplest daily routines, including taking the kids to school. It was a crutch I needed to get around town and back home at the end of the day.

Not only were there occasions of unknowingly becoming lost in my own mind, but there were also times I needed to purposely remove myself, mentally, from reality. One vivid memory I have of doing this was when my mom's husband died just a few months after Mark. I wanted to be there for her, help her, support her, but my brain was still in fight or flight mode. Flight mode spared me from temporary pain, and I didn't question when it kicked in. At the visitation for Tom, I kept finding excuses to come and go. Although I didn't realize it at the time, I now know I was doing what I had to do to survive. It wasn't until years later in my grief recovery journey that I recognized what I had done and the reasons behind it. I felt I needed to be there, so I was for short bursts of time, and then I would remove myself to focus on some other task I deemed necessary at the time. I was trying to justify my exits during a difficult time for my mom.

The funeral was held at the same church where Mark's funeral was. I hadn't been back to that church since then. Sitting in that front row with my mom brought back a rockslide of emotions, but I couldn't escape this time. I wanted to scream and had an intense desire to get up and run. My body actually kept moving forward as if getting ready to stand. I would have to tense my muscles and hold my breath to stay in my seat. I've experienced no greater moment of self-control as I did that day.

I also learned how powerful the human brain is while I forced myself to stay in that church. I was in a mental state that I could not withstand, almost as though I would explode if the pressure were not immediately released. To ground myself, I sat back in the pew where my face would be in the stream of sunlight coming in through the window, and I visualized myself on a beach. In my mind's eye, I felt the warmth of the sun on my skin and grains of sand between my toes and under my feet. I slowed my breathing to take in the scent of the ocean. I heard the sound of the waves rolling in and the seagulls squawking as they flew by. I tasted the salted air on my lips. All my senses were heightened to enjoy my favorite happy place. My body relaxed the painful grip it had on me, and my mind completely drowned out my uncomfortable reality. Never in my life had I been so completely transported through the power of my own mind. This worked so well that I have continued to call upon the power of my mind to alter various situations I encounter and to bring about positive realities.

There is nothing more amazing or powerful than learning to control your thoughts. When you control your thoughts, you control your life. But the mind is a muscle that needs continual exercise. If you don't practice controlling your thoughts on a daily basis, the power is greatly weakened and quickly lost. For me, it's a practice worth taking the time for.

CHAPTER 15
A GRIEVING FAMILY'S BEST FRIEND

"There is no better example of unconditional love than the love of a dog for his people." – Patty Slupecki

He stood eye to eye with Jake, weighed in at a solid hundred pounds, and was black as night. Bo was our Labrador, truly a gentle giant of a dog. He would back Jake up against the hallway closet doors by licking Jake's face. I'd like to think it was a way of showing his love for one of his people, but it may have been the food left on the four-year-old's face after a snack. Jake would shake his head from side to side, giggling and calling out 'Moooommm' as if he needed rescuing.

Bo was a great dog, easily trained, and very obedient. The kitchen counter was right at his nose level, yet he never swiped any food. I could leave a platter of meat on the bench outside while Mark prepped the grill for a cookout, tell Bo 'No,' and he wouldn't touch it. He was near perfect with one-word commands like sit, down, and stay. He was always so excited when the doorbell rang, believing visitors arrived just to pet and play with him, but that bouncing, tail-wagging, four-legged giant could be intimidating to the non-dog loving types. The simple command, 'kennel' sent Bo directly to his crate where he stayed until he heard the command, 'free'.

Bo was the perfect family pet, full of energy, tolerant, and ready to play with kids at any moment. Jake could ride on his back as if riding a horse and Ellie thought it was fun to yell out commands as fast as she could to see if Bo could keep up…he did! He followed me everywhere I went, including when it was bedtime. No matter what activity was going on in the house, Bo was there. When I went to bed, Bo followed me and slept under my bed until I got up.

After Mark died, Bo changed his habits and demeanor. He seemed to know that Mark was gone, and I believe he mourned Mark. I kept Bo's food in a large wheeled container in the garage just outside the laundry room door. One morning, when I went to fill Bo's bowl with his breakfast, he followed me all the way into the garage and retrieved one of Mark's running shoes. I had required those smelly shoes stay out of the house, so Mark had created a landing spot in the garage for all things sweaty and smelly. I hadn't yet had the strength to move any of those belongings. Bo carried that laced-up, blue and grey shoe around with him for weeks, never chewing it up, just keeping it with him. Previously, Bo had been known to chew on shoes or stuffed animals if they were left out and accessible. He stopped doing that altogether. Weird.

Bo also became our protector in extraordinary ways. Bo became wary of visitors and their intentions. No longer so excited to interact with unfamiliar people, he would plant himself squarely between the kids, me, and any unusual visitor. He was very protective of us especially if a man came to the house. One time, my friend, Paul, stopped by as he did from time to time. Bo knew him, but this time when Paul leaned in to offer me a hug, Bo growled at him. That was completely out of character, but it was clear that my big black lab was taking his newly adopted role as the household protector seriously.

After Mark died, Bo no longer followed me to bed or slept under my bed at night. He stayed downstairs until the last of the three of us climbed the stairs for the night. Once we were all tucked in, Bo rotated between each of our bedrooms, staying in the hallway but lying in front of each door for a short while before moving to the next. If one of us got up during the night, Bo would move to the landing at the top of the steps as if he were guarding the entire second floor of the house. This routine continued for years.

When Bo sensed that one of us was having a difficult time, he would position himself next to us and lay his large head in our lap. His silent support lasted until we made the first move. While his head may be resting on us, he didn't nap during these periods of time. His eyes remained open, occasionally scanning the room, still keeping an eye on our surroundings.

Bo started following all three of us. When any of us moved, Bo went along to check things out. Even during the day and between his naps, Bo would circulate through the house to find each of us and then return to a centralized location. He always seemed to be watching over us. In many ways, he was our caretaker, and I felt safer with Bo around.

As Bo got older, I dreaded the day he would die and prayed that none of us would have to find him unresponsive in our home. My fear was that when our protector left us, our grieving for Mark would be brought back to the surface. As it turned out, Bo lived to be 15, and Jake and I were with him when the vet needed to put him down. It was a tough experience for sure, but his health had deteriorated to the point he could not stand on his own. After trying all we could, we couldn't let him suffer any more. Now we talk about Bo almost as often as we talk about Mark.

CHAPTER 16
THE AUTOPSY REPORT

"Holding on to negative emotions keeps you stuck. Choosing to let go of negative emotions frees you to move forward." - Patty Slupecki

On a warm fall day, a hand-addressed, business-sized envelope arrived in the mail. The writing was familiar, but it didn't initially register with me. The return address label had Mark's name on it. I was puzzled, thrown for a minute. Was this from Mark? How could it be? What was it? I had this entire conversation with myself in the time it took me to walk from the mailbox to the front door. I stared at it for a minute until I realized it was my own hand writing on a self-addressed stamped envelope. I couldn't recall what it was for. I tore open the envelope as soon as I got into the office. Inside was a single sheet of paper. I unfolded it to reveal a photocopied letterhead from the County Coroner's Office. The subject line: *Case Summary of the Death of Mark Slupecki.* I took a hard swallow of emotion, braced myself, and continued reading.

The details of blunt force injuries were listed, and the coroner's conclusion read:

"It is my opinion that Mark Slupecki died of blunt force

injuries of chest and pelvis due to bicyclist vs. pickup truck. Manner of death: accident – bicyclist on bike trail, struck by pickup truck."

Tears flooded my eyes and blurred my vision, then audible sobs escaped from within me as I read through the list of traumatic injuries that Mark sustained. I didn't even understand what some of the medical terms meant, but I understood enough to come completely unglued.

I was home alone; the kids were in school. I didn't think; I instinctively picked up the phone and called Mike at work. His assistant answered the phone, and I don't think she understood anything I said because I was so hysterical. Thankfully, Mike had instructed her to always locate him when I called and put my calls through. She explained that Mike was in a meeting, but she wanted me to stay on the line while she went to get him. In short order, Mike was on the phone with me. I'm sure he was just as devastated as I was when I conveyed the details of the autopsy report, but he contained his emotion and was a rock for me. We stayed on the line for some time, mostly in silence, as we both struggled to digest the graphic details.

At the time, I did not question why a toxicology report was run as part of the autopsy. I assumed it was standard procedure, and maybe it is, but what I learned several weeks later made my blood boil.

Uncle had made arrangements to get a copy of the accident report, complete with photographs. He had the good sense to have the information delivered to himself so as not to blindside me with more vivid images and descriptions of the horrific accident. He softened the blow by first telling me that he *had* the information in his possession. Then he explained what was included in small, manageable doses to prepare me for the details I would read. He also described the photographs and warned me that in one picture, taken at a distance, Mark was lying in the ditch surrounded by first responders. After delivering the information as gently as he could, Uncle handed me a large, thick envelope and suggested I put it aside until I was ready to look at its contents.

I waited until I was alone before looking inside the envelope. When I opened it, I found a multi-page Traffic Crash Report and a secondary envelope that contained the photographs. At first, fear kept me from opening the paper-wrapped stack of photos. I decided to start with the report. I scanned it initially, confirming what Uncle had prepared me for. Then, I went back through each page, reading every word, sometimes more than once. I needed to understand what happened; I was looking for answers. My heart raced, and my hands shook as I held the papers.

Pages of details were outlined: traffic, road conditions, weather, cornfield obstruction, vehicle damage, and injuries. Okay, I thought. These are straightforward facts, nothing unexpected here. Moving on through the stapled packet, I saw a sketch with labels including: gouges and scrapes, skid marks, bicycle, blood splatter, shoe, bike seat, second shoe, and, final resting spot of bicyclist. I think I must have been holding my breath at this point because I felt pressure building inside my chest and let it out in a long, loud puff of air.

Another page laid out the minute by minute course of events from the time of the first 911 call to the clearing of the scene, and finally, notification of next of kin. I realized, somewhat disassociated from what I was reading, that was me. The timeline described the arrival of the County Sheriff's Department, State Highway Patrol, City EMS, Advance Life Support Team, and the Critical Care Helicopter Transport. Every law enforcement officer's name was listed with the corresponding time of arrival and time they cleared the scene. The narrative section of the report described the officer's interaction with the medical teams and hospital personnel along with his summary and opinions regarding the accident.

The narrative noted that the first call for help came in at 2:18 pm. It was *2:15 pm* when I was startled awake from my nap on the couch with Jake. I don't believe that this is a coincidence. I don't know exactly what woke me up so suddenly, but something abruptly altered my state of consciousness at, what must have been, the moment of Mark's accident.

I continued poring over the timeline and details, thinking back and trying to match up where I was and what I was doing to the accident timeline. 2:57 pm was identified as the time the helicopter left the scene with "the patient." It is also noted that the hospital confirmed the "victim expired" at 3:38 pm and that Patricia Slupecki identified the body at 5:50 pm. These notes referred to Mark and me; it seemed unreal, a mistake. This kind of tragedy couldn't have really happened to us. We were young, happy, healthy, and had so much life to live. But sadly, this was our story. It was surprising to me how much time elapsed from when I got up from my nap to when I identified the body of my dead husband. My whole world had stopped that day and left me suspended in time.

Two investigations were conducted, one by law enforcement and the second by my insurance company. It took several weeks for the insurance company to complete and report their findings. There were discrepancies and differing opinions about how the accident occurred. Complicated factors delayed the progress: First, bystanders at the accident moved Mark's bicycle and the accident debris from the road before authorities arrived. Second, the cornfields noted in the accident report as obstructing the view to both the bicyclist and the pickup truck driver were mowed down before investigators visited the site. Lastly, the pickup truck driver's insurance company was not responding to inquiries. It was through a series of phone calls with several individuals that the details were eventually revealed to me. This is when I learned that the driver of the pickup truck that killed Mark had lied to police. He gave false insurance information to the authorities at the scene and in the official accident report. In fact, the man who ended the life of my children's father was an uninsured motorist. The police findings were based largely on the pickup truck driver's statement. A copy of his handwritten statement was included with the packet I received from Uncle.

In part, the statement read:
> "...out of the blue a cyclist smashed into [my] windshield...I did not see him at all. I don't know what happened. I don't know [if he was stopped] I never [saw] him until I saw his face on my windshield."

A drawing was included with the pickup truck driver's statement as well. I found it interesting that it looks *exactly* like the sketch from the investigating officer's Traffic Crash Report. Another interesting piece of information revealed to me was that NO toxicology report was done on the pickup truck driver. This is where my blood still boils. The lying, uninsured driver that killed Mark was never tested for drugs or alcohol, but the dead body of my husband was tested.

I believe there were missteps in the way the investigations were conducted, and I'm not alone in that belief. The initial and only police report, dated the day of the accident, states that Mark "failed to stop for a posted stop sign." However, there were no witnesses, and even the pickup truck driver himself stated that he didn't know whether or not Mark had stopped.

Family members talked to attorneys and had researched and gathered a significant amount of intel. They made recommendations to me on how best to proceed, but, in the end, I decided not to pursue legal action. My children and I had far more to lose than the man that killed Mark did. Our lives were ripped to shreds and have forever been changed in ways I can't begin to describe. A lawsuit would have only prolonged and intensified our pain. The only thing I wanted was to have Mark back, and that was the one outcome I could never be awarded.

I made a conscious decision to let go of the accident questions that haunted me and to let go of my intense anger at the pickup truck driver and the mishandled investigation. It would not serve me in any way to hold onto these ill feelings or to keep asking myself 'why.' I needed my strength and energy to survive this great loss, and as the only parent left to raise two young children, I needed to focus on their well-being. So again, I used the power of my own mind and sheer determination to eliminate these thoughts. I packed away the autopsy, police report, investigation papers, and photos both figuratively and literally. It wasn't until writing this book, nearly 16 years later, that I opened and reread these files.

I have no regrets, nor have I second-guessed my decision. It's out my hands, and I'm okay with that.

CHAPTER 17
THE FIRST CHRISTMAS

"Small, thoughtful gestures can often be more meaningful and memorable than the most grandiose shows of kindness." – Patty Slupecki

We had been a family of three for only a few months when the holidays rolled in. If it had been up to me, I would have let them roll by without any acknowledgement. I was concerned that carrying on with our holiday traditions would only intensify the fact that Mark was missing. I just didn't see how I could bear it, but having young children meant that ignoring the biggest holiday of the year was not an option for me. Santa would never forget children on Christmas, especially not Jake and Ellie this year.

Thankfully, my sister came to the rescue once again and said we would catalog shop this year. I thought that was a great idea. It would spare me from having to step foot inside stores that would be decorated for the holidays and filled with happy families shopping together. Just the thought of having to see that caused a spike in my anxiety level.

Sue gave me a catalog from a small, locally-owned toy store and told me to circle the things I wanted to get for Ellie and Jake. We used to do that as kids ourselves when the Sears Wish Book catalog came out in the fall. I did as she suggested and put an initial by each item, just like we did as grade-schoolers, to clearly identify what each of the kids wanted. Sue called the store to explain the situation. They were incredibly accommodating, took the order over the phone, then wrapped and labeled all of the gifts for each of the kids. The presents were ready to pick up a couple days later, and I didn't even have to go inside the store. The owner met me at the back door and helped me load everything into my car. This is another example of someone going out of their way to do something kind for me, for no reason other than to make the holidays a bit more tolerable. While my holiday shopping task may seem insignificant to others, this truly was a great burden lifted from my shoulders. I was still just going through the motions of life, but not living, and holiday preparations would only add to my burden.

When Mark was alive, putting up the Christmas tree had been a fun family evening complete with hot chocolate and marshmallows. Sue knew it was important for my kids to have a Christmas tree and was well aware of how difficult it would be for me, so, she changed things up. Sue and her family came over to complete the task with us. The kids had some fun, and I wasn't alone, one more Christmas complete.

My favorite holiday tradition was a simple act of kindness that Mark bestowed on me not only on Christmas but on all the major holidays including my birthday and Mother's Day. He would get up first, make the coffee, open a bottle of champagne to make mimosas, and then deliver both to me in bed. There may have only been time for me to have a sip or two before the kids were up, but I enjoyed and appreciated the tradition every time.

Mike and Sharie, along with their three kids, came into town for Christmas and stayed at my house for the holiday week. They altered their own family traditions so my kids and I would not be alone on Christmas morning. This was a first for us but became a new and wonderful tradition of spending holidays together and even vacationing together as families.

On Christmas morning the kids were happy and excited, no doubt because their cousins were with them and Santa had indeed found them all. When I went downstairs after being dragged out of bed by the kids, Mike met me with a cup of coffee and a mimosa. I didn't even remember telling him the story about how Mark would do this for me. Writing this, even now, brings a happy tear to my eye. This was one of most thoughtful things anyone has ever done for me.

Snow began falling as the kids opened their gifts, and even I had to admit it was beautiful. Mike's kids were jumping up and down with excitement because living in Florida didn't give them any opportunities to experience snow. The rush of activity and sounds of enthusiastic children distracted me from the agony I felt inside. I had to go searching for winter hats, gloves, and boots for Mike's kids to wear as there was no need for them to own these items. As I dug through the closet, I found Mark's winter outerwear and offered it to Mike.

When all the Floridians were layered up as best they could be, Mike headed outside with all the kids and a shovel. Sharie and I watched from the living room window as snow continued falling harder and faster. It did bring me a bit of joy to watch them all having so much fun, especially Jake and Ellie. I was grateful to have a house full of people breathing a little life back into my home. Mike, forever a kid at heart, was right in the middle of all the fun but in between still found time to shovel the driveway. As soon as he got to the bottom of the driveway, the snow was already piled up again at the top, and he would have to start over. Finally, Mike dropped the shovel into the snow, raised his arms and eyes to the sky and yelled, "Enough Mark! I'm done with the snow." From inside, we girls were enjoying the comedy of it, and really, Mike was too.

As the years went by and Jake got older and more capable in the kitchen, he took over the coffee and champagne tradition and continued it until he grew up and moved out on his own. In the early years, it started with me getting everything set up for him the night before and then talking him through the process in the morning, but he wanted to do it on his own and he did. Even as he became a teenager who regularly slept half the day away, he didn't miss a holiday. He set an alarm on his own and delivered the liquid traditions just as planned. I smile, thinking how such a simple act of kindness can leave a lasting imprint on one's heart. This ranks as another one of the most caring things anyone has ever done for me. Mark would be so proud.

CHAPTER 18
BEAT THE BUS

"You are capable of reaching heights greater than your wildest dreams have ever imagined." – Patty Slupecki

Mark was an avid runner and competed in marathons, triathlons, and countless 5 and 10K races every year. Mike had reached out to Mark just a week before he died to talk about running. Mike was interested in beginning a running routine and was seeking some guidance. The two made a plan to run The Seven Mile Bridge Race together in the Spring of 2003. The race is an annual event in the Florida Keys, entirely over water, and limited to just 1,500 participants. Runners must complete the race within 90 minutes or be picked up by yellow school buses that reopen the only road that leads in and out of the Keys.

Mark's passion for running was complicated by the fact he was an insulin dependent diabetic. This, and his Type A perfectionism, led Mark to maintain a detailed running journal and blood sugar log. He had volumes of spiral-bound books filled with the details of each run: times, distance, hydration, nutrition, sugar intake, and blood sugar levels. Complicated formulas were laid out to maintain the correct balance of all these details which, of course, would allow

Mark to reach and exceed his goals.

I don't get running nor did I particularly enjoy watching other people run. However, because it was important to Mark, I supported his daily runs after work and cheered him on at all the weekend races although I must admit, I wasn't always offering support with a smile or a pleasant attitude.

I expected payback. I wanted time off from parenting to pursue my own interests on occasion and I did…while Mark was alive. He was always completely supportive of my scrapbook weekends away and my annual girls vacation. He cheered me on as I played doubles on a local tennis team and happily stayed home with the kids while I participated in monthly Bunco and mom's night out groups.

Yes, he really was that awesome. I wish I would have appreciated him more when he was alive. Why did I not realize how blessed I was to have this man as my husband and the father of my children until he was gone? Why didn't I tell him more often how great he was?

During a conversation in the days before the funeral, Mike shared the details of the plan to run the 2003 Seven Mile Bridge Race that he and Mark had discussed just one week earlier. Mike said he was still going to run the race, for Mark. A warm feeling and a sense of comfort came over me; I was touched by Mike's desire to honor his brother in this way.

Mike, Sharie, and I continued to sit in silence together. Through the numbness, an idea pushed its way to my consciousness. I said I would run with him; we could do it together. My eyes darted over to Sharie, and I blurted out that we all would run with him. Sharie looked at me wide-eyed, probably questioning my sanity at the moment. None of us were runners. We would need to start from square one.

Mike became our leader and in short order the five of us, Mark's two brothers, their wives, and me, were committed to running the race as a way to honor Mark. I think it also gave us a goal to focus on, something we could do, achieve, and look forward to during what would surely be a very dark year.

After the funeral was over, Mike packed up Mark's running journals and books to take home. He was going to learn everything he could about how Mark trained and how to beat Mark's time.

Training for the race would need to happen on our own as we all lived in different areas of the country. Mike researched and created a training plan for us to follow. Seven miles doesn't sound all that far, but for our tribe of non-runners it was a Mount Everest kind of challenge.

I began running, well sort of running, within a few weeks. My distance was measured by mailboxes. 'I'll run twelve mailboxes,' I told myself on training day one. I put on an old pair of shorts and one of Mark's running tees from a race he had completed. I tied up my laces in a double knot, thinking of the tripping hazard I should avoid on my first run. The front door closed behind me and I was off.

Feeling pretty good, I walked to the corner of my cul-de-sac where I could see a good long stretch of road and started counting. 'Shit!' I can't even see twelve mailboxes in front of me; perhaps I set my goal a bit high. 'Walk to the first one and then start running,' I told myself.

Mailbox one - go! I ran five mailboxes, my chest heaving and droplets of sweat building on my forehead. Then I walked for the next twenty-five boxes to catch my breath. 'That's enough for today!' I decided and strolled back home.

An adjusted plan was created to aid in my success, and I tried again. Walk three boxes, run three boxes. Walk three boxes, run four boxes. Walk three boxes, run five boxes. The pattern continued over the next weeks until I was able to measure my distance by miles.

Sharie did all the research on the Seven Mile Bridge Race. There were limited spots available due to safety concerns on the segmental bridge that stretches between Knights and Little Duck Keys. The entrance process was via a postal lottery. It was 2003, so online registrations were not available.

Interested participants needed to send a self-addressed, stamped envelope to the Marathon Running Club by a certain date. Then on a later predetermined date the Club would mail out the registration forms all at once to those who had sent in the required envelope ahead of time. Only one application per envelope was permitted. The first 1,500 people to return the application were awarded a coveted spot in the race.

We were a little concerned about getting into the race together, so Sharie took charge of the entire process for all five of us. She and Mike live in Florida, the rest of us did not, so it seemed to reason that having a Florida address would give us a timing/distance advantage with the mail delivery.

Sharie used her address for all the correspondence and later for the applications. She watched the mail closely, filled out all the applications, wrote separate checks for each one, and mailed them all back immediately to give us our best shot at getting in. We were on pins and needles waiting to hear; all of us needed to get in. We needed to run this race together, for Mark.

The first public display of my newly developed ability to run came on Thanksgiving morning 2002. The annual Turkey Trot 5K was routed through my neighborhood, and this year I was no longer a spectator. Family and friends gathered at my house, some to run with me, some to cheer, and some to have breakfast and champagne ready when we completed the race.

I was a bit nervous and a bit excited. Mark would be so proud of me for running, and I was proud of myself for trying, for training, and for staying committed to my goal. I had a few butterflies in my stomach and worried about having to go to the bathroom during the race. I decided to forgo my morning coffee just to be safe.

About twenty minutes before the race was to begin, I left my house, entourage in tow. The starting line was just around the corner from my house, so we all walked there together. The closer we got, the louder the music. There were people everywhere, some jogging in place, others chatting, and a few wearing turkey head hats. I had to gently push my way through the crowd, ducking past conversations, shimmying through narrow gaps, and saying 'excuse me' every few steps. As a new runner, I worked my way to the back third of the crowd, lining up behind the starting gate, and took my spot in the back of the pack where I thought I wouldn't get trampled.

The gun went off and my first race was underway...well almost. I had to wait a couple of minutes for the wave of runners ahead of me to get going. Then, I was off and running. Uncle and Mark's best friend from high school ran by my side the entire way even though they were both capable of running a much better time than I was.

It was a cold morning and in short order my breathing became heavy and noisy, but my team kept me going. About half way into the race my energy was running on reserves. As we rounded another curve, I breathlessly asked Uncle "Are we going uphill?" He burst into laughter.

We live in the Midwest where the topography is flat as a pancake. For a seasoned athlete like Uncle, the 'hill' in question was nonexistent. Actually, if I had been walking, I may not have noticed the slight incline either. I sucked it up, embarrassed, and kept going.

The support and encouragement were plentiful. Friends and neighbors were in their front yards waiting for me to pass. They held up signs, yelled, and made me beam from ear to ear. It kept me moving. Those were the fun moments.

I crossed the finish line and suddenly felt a surge of renewed energy. I completed a 5K without stopping once! I was relieved and felt confident about being able to run seven miles in April.

My training continued through the coldest winter months. My breathing never seemed to get any better even though my physical conditioning was vastly improved. I was curious about this, but not bothered enough to ask any questions.

After one particular late morning training run, I opened my front door and was glad to be back in my warm house. My running leggings and top layers were sweaty, but I was still cold. Having completed a four mile run, I was feeling pretty good. I peeled off my outer fleece just as the phone rang.

Caller ID told me it was Sharie calling so I answered. "We're in! We're ALL in!" she said, barely giving me the chance to say hello. Excitement filled our conversation. Sharie had successfully navigated the postal lottery, and all five of us were registered and accepted into the 21st Annual Seven Mile Bridge Race.

When I hung up the phone I sank into a chair at the kitchen table, suddenly feeling somewhat guilty. I hadn't felt much excitement in the past several months since Mark died. How could I be excited now about a race when he wasn't here to participate? Running was his passion, not mine. He planned to do this race with his brother, not me.

Tears filled my eyes and ran down my cheeks. For a while, grief hit me with the force of a truck, like the truck that killed Mark. My chest hurt, the gaping hole of grief was imploding into my core, and my head throbbed. I just wanted him back.

Throughout our training, we all shared the same fear: if we didn't finish the race in the allotted amount of time, we would be picked up by the bus. None of us wanted to ride the bus of shame. Our motto became 'beat the bus.'

When April finally arrived, we were all feeling good about our ability to complete the race. We started out together and then fanned out at our own pace. It was a hot and sunny race day. At the top of the bridge, fire trucks were spraying water across the lanes of runners like a giant sprinkler. I had been training in Ohio winter weather conditions, so the heat was hitting me pretty hard. The cool water was a welcome relief if only for a moment. I couldn't stop to enjoy it; I had already fallen to the back of the pack. I had to keep moving; I had to beat the bus.

Mike, Andy, Marge, and Sharie crossed the finish line ahead of me; they beat the bus. Mike came back to finish the race with me. I was close. I could see the finish line and banner that spanned across the bridge. Mike had carried a camera with him to take pictures during the race. He was cheering me on and snapping some pictures of me. I turned around to look behind me. I saw more runners that were followed by the yellow school buses. Ahead of me, in the distance, I could see the race workers starting to disassemble the finish line banner. 'I've got this,' I told myself and continued running.

Mike had sprinted ahead to snap some pictures of me. In the first photo, I was near the finish line and the banner was coming down on one side. In the second photo, I crossed the finish line and the banner was almost down on the second side. I did it. I crossed the finish line on my own two feet. I beat the bus!

CHAPTER 19
BREATHING IS A NECESSITY

"Listen to your own body; it tells you everything you need to know."
– Patty Slupecki

Experiencing the traumatic event of Mark's death catapulted me into an emotional turmoil that I was unequipped to deal with. In addition to being sucked into a deep depression, I believe the immobilizing upheaval in my life exhibited itself physically although it would take quite some time for me to recognize what was happening. Slowly and methodically, without my conscious awareness, my body began to attack itself. As a result, I developed an extremely rare autoimmune disease called Idiopathic Subglottic Tracheal Stenosis.

This condition is an internal narrowing of the airway below the vocal cords. Scar tissue builds up in a circular direction causing the trachea or airway to become gradually narrower over time, making it increasingly difficult to breathe. Thus, the autoimmune disease – the body attacks itself and tries to kill off good tissue by mistake.

In my case, the cause is idiopathic, meaning the medical

community has no explanation or reason for this happening. I know why it happened to me; it's my body's reaction to, or way of dealing with, the emotional trauma I've been subjected to. This makes complete sense to me. However, the scientific - thinking doctors haven't yet agreed with me. Not only did grief exhibit itself through health issues with me, but both of Mark's parents developed major health issues that spiraled out of control after his death. These issues eventually led to both of their deaths. Even my children's health was seriously affected, leaving them with lingering issues as well. There is no coincidence here.

When I started running to train for the Seven Mile Bridge Race, I began to notice difficulty with my breathing. I assumed it was a natural occurrence associated with physical exertion and the challenge to my body. I reasoned that every runner breathed hard and was out of breath during their run. Therefore, I was fine and ignored the messages my body was sending me.

Over the course of the year following the race, my symptoms became increasingly noticeable and worrisome. Surviving widowhood and raising my children alone still consumed me, and although I didn't care so much about my own well-being, I did care about my kids. I was the only parent they had. They needed me, so I had to be okay; I had to be healthy.

My breathing went from bad to worse, and others were starting to notice and comment on the noisiness of my breathing. Simply reading a children's storybook aloud caused me to stop and catch my breath. It was time to seek medical intervention.

I made several doctor visits and tried a number of medications, all of which failed to help. I was diagnosed with asthma, and then told my symptoms were caused by anxiety. By this point in time, another year had passed. I was frustrated, annoyed, and tried to just ignore the situation. But, gradually, panic began to build with my inability to breathe normally. Something was really wrong. I didn't want the kids to see my concern or worry about something happening to me, so I decided to go to the ER. There, I relayed my entire story and finished by asserting that the inhaler doesn't work. It didn't make breathing any easier or quieter. "Yes, it does," Replied the attending physician in a condescending tone. "It's your imagination."

At that time in my life, I was insecure, self-conscious, and allowed myself to be put down. I felt small and insignificant. I questioned myself. 'Was I making up this entire ordeal?' I didn't think so, but this man was a doctor; surely, he knew better than me. Today, my confident, secure, independent self says 'BULLSHIT!' I did know better. I intuitively knew there was something wrong in my body. Doctors practice medicine; that's right, they don't know medicine, they practice it. I knew my body.

Back in the ER, the attending physician ordered a bronchoscopy. My situation wasn't deemed an emergency, so the procedure was scheduled for the next day and I was sent home with another inhaler.

I spent the evening wondering if that ER doctor was right. I felt bad about myself, my life, my situation. I was overwhelmed by thoughts of 'Why me? It's not fair. What did I do to deserve all this? I want Mark back. I can't do this.' After the kids were tucked into bed, I opened a bottle of wine and kept drinking until the bottle ran dry. I had worked myself into a death spiral, lying on the floor in Mark's office. My eyes were nearly swollen shut; my tee was soaked from the flood of tears, and I was breathing so hard I could feel my heartbeat throbbing through my entire body.

It was a long night. When the morning finally arrived, I put on my fake happy face for the kids' sake. I would not let them know how miserable I felt. I had to keep them moving forward. Sometimes it was all I could do to keep myself upright. Keeping an object in motion tends to take far less energy than stopping and starting again. This was how I felt about the kids. It tore me apart to deal with their meltdowns and outbursts of grief. Sometimes it was easier to just keep them going, moving, doing. This was one of those days. I needed to avoid any additional stress on myself by having to deal with a kid issue or I might implode.

I feel guilty about my selfishness and thought twice before admitting it to the world, but, my intention is to help other people feel less alone in their grief journey. Was I being a bad mom? No, I was being a real mom, a grief-stricken mom, suffering through my own pain and trying to do the best with the hand I was dealt.

After I dropped the kids off at school, my mom took me to the hospital where the bronchoscopy was performed under anesthesia. The procedure took mere minutes because the doctor had never seen anything like this. He immediately referred me to an ENT (an ear, nose, and throat doctor) who was willing to see me the next day.

It was a Friday night in December 2005 when I arrived for my 5:00 pm ENT appointment. There was no one in the office, and some of the lights were already off. The doctor was the only person there, waiting to see me before going to his holiday party. He met me at the front door, and we walked together back to an exam room. I was feeling appreciative and thanked him profusely for making the time to see me.

As instructed, I sat in the exam chair, straight and tall, chin up. The doctor wore one of those funny looking, mirrored headlamp things and squinted one eye shut. He wrapped my tongue in gauze and pulled it out of the way so he could look down my throat. I gagged as he placed a flexible instrument into place. He let up a moment later and asked if I was okay. I shook my head and tried to focus on relaxing my neck and jaw while praying I wouldn't throw up.

The handsome, very kind doctor stepped back and began asking questions as he removed his gloves and the elastic band from his head. "So, this is quite uncommon, and there aren't any physicians locally who can deal with this issue." 'Uncommon,' I thought. 'Well that suits me perfectly. I once had to have a piece of apple peel surgically removed from one of my tonsils!' "Your airway is very narrow, which is why you are having so much difficulty breathing. I have a friend from medical school who is an Otolaryngologist, a head and neck surgeon, up at the University of Michigan. I'm going to give her a call."

Right there, in the exam room with me listening, he pulled out his cell phone and made the call. Amazing! This guy was really going above and beyond for me. All the planets must have been aligned that evening because that med school friend answered her phone. They briefly discussed my situation, and the call ended. "I want you to be up at U of M on Monday, first thing in the morning. Dr. Kara will see you when you get there." I asked what time my appointment was scheduled. "It doesn't matter, get there as early as you can and she will see you right away," he instructed.

'Wow' I thought. I must not be crazy. Something really is wrong, and I am finally with doctors who get it and really care. The ENT physician explained where I should go and even gave me directions to get there. "Now, I want you to go home and stay there all weekend. Don't do anything physical - no cleaning, no shoveling snow, no going up and down the steps. I want you to sit on the couch and watch television all weekend. If your symptoms get worse, go immediately to the closest ER and tell them to call me."

I did just as I was told but wasn't too concerned. I thought the doctor was just being cautious. On Monday morning, my mom came over to the house to get the kids off to school and my sister and my mother-in-law took me to U of M.

As we pulled onto the hospital campus, my eyes widened, taking in the vastness of the facility. We didn't have hospitals that big in Toledo. I wondered how the heck we would figure out which way to go. There were so many different buildings and more directional signs than I could read as we passed by. After parking near the top of the parking garage, it took the three of us about 15 minutes to meander our way through walkways to the Otolaryngology Department. The waiting room was already full of people and it was only 8:00 am. The check-in desk was across the long, narrow room opposite the door where we entered. My eyes scanned the area quickly, noticing several things that gave me a clear indication of what an Otolaryngologist specialized in, and it made me feel a little queasy. I saw a young man in a wheelchair with metal rods screwed into his skull, an older gentleman with only half a face, and others with white bandages wrapped around their head, neck, or face. Oh my God, could this happen to me too? By the time I reached the desk to sign in, I was worried and felt sick to my stomach.

I don't handle medical issues well. I don't like to be around sick people or see bodily fluids. In fact, I am so affected by these things that as preschoolers, my children learned that every room in our home contained a pre-lined throw up bucket. If they were going to vomit, they had to do it in the bucket and tie up the bag for me. Otherwise, I would be joining the vomit party.

I only had to wait a few minutes before being called back to an exam room. Sue and Pat followed me in. I was quite nervous and needed the moral support in the uncomfortable atmosphere. Dr. Kara entered the room right away and introduced herself. She was a middle-aged woman with blonde hair and a pretty face. She looked like a friend to me and treated me like one too. That put me more at ease.

She performed a bronchoscopy right there in the exam room with only numbing spray squirted into my nostrils and down my throat. This was the same procedure that just four days earlier had required a sterilized hospital procedure room and anesthesia in Toledo. Again, I answered a lot of questions. "No, I've never been intubated, never had any surgeries, never had been in any accidents, never smoked, never had cancer. I don't have any diseases, reflux, or any other health problems. The only medication I take is an antidepressant."

Dr. Kara explained that she had never seen a patient with such a narrow airway that could not be explained by previous injury to the trachea. She excused herself to confer with her colleagues in the department. My nerves were kicking in again, and my bladder needed emptying. I walked down the hall to find a restroom and as I turned the corner, I could see Dr. Kara talking with four or five other people, all wearing white coats. 'Were they talking about me?' I wondered but was not self-conscious about it. I was more concerned with what was wrong with me and why it took so many people to figure it out.

My internal temperature was rising parallel to my nerves, and I felt the need to remove a winter layer of clothing. Sue and Pat tried to distract me with random conversation. When the surgeon returned to the exam room, she asked, "What did you eat for breakfast this morning?" "A bowl of Cheerios and black coffee. Why?" She explained the consensus she and her colleagues had come to; they felt my trachea was not stable enough to perform surgery without first performing a tracheotomy. She said she wanted to take me into surgery immediately and went on to explain the details of the procedure and what I could expect. "Once the tracheotomy is complete, we will give you the happy juice and you'll drift off to sleep. We will make several incisions with a laser through the scar tissue that is built up inside your airway. Then we'll inject steroids into the incisions and a balloon will be inserted and pumped up to stretch the airway. Finally, a topical application of Mitomycin C, a chemotherapy drug, will be swabbed into the incisions."

I had what seemed like hundreds of questions and so did my

sister and mother-in-law. Mostly, I was worried about my kids. After Mark died, I promised them I would always come home. In hindsight, this wasn't a very good idea, but when my children panicked at the thought of me never coming home like Daddy, I promised anything to ease their fear. After explaining my story to a very patient, caring Dr. Kara, she suggested I call the school and ask to speak to the kids myself. This was a brilliant idea. I was able to explain things to them; they asked me questions and heard me answer. I gave the performance of my life and they were none the wiser. After the surgery, I would be left with a hole in my neck from where I would have to breathe, and I would be unable to talk.

'Shit! Seriously God, I want off this damn merry-go-round.'

Hospital transport refused to take me to the Pre-Op area. It seems that as soon as the medical community knows you're an airway patient, a red flag goes up. There is a great concern for a possible collapsed airway and the need for immediate intervention. No one is too keen on dealing with that situation. Dr. Kara introduced me to her resident, a wonderful young man and truly caring like Dr. Kara. He would personally take me to the pre-op area while Dr. Kara cleared her schedule and transferred her patients to the other surgeons willing to step in and help. All of these people were going out of their way, big time, to help me and other patients were being inconvenienced and maybe even disappointed because of me. I wondered, 'Do they know they helped save my life that day? Do they know they helped a widowed mom return to her children? Do they have any idea the level of appreciation I have for them?'

The resident asked if I needed a wheelchair. "No, can I just walk with you?" He smiled and nodded his head in approval. One of the nurses explained to my sister and mother-in-law where they would need to go to wait for me. They both hugged me before I followed the resident to the pre-op area.

It felt odd to walk into the long, bed-lined area wearing my regular clothes, knowing I was the patient. The other patients we passed by were tied up in hospital gowns, lying on wheeled beds underneath white blankets. I had never seen so many hospital beds in one area; they continued beyond where I could see. Each bed was separated by a curtain that hung from a track in the ceiling. There were no chairs next to the beds, only medical equipment. Visitors were not permitted in this area. Uniformed medical staff were bustling around at what seemed like a frantic pace. Buzzers and beepers were sounding off all around me along with monotone medical chatter. I stuck out in my street clothes.

A tall, muscular man dressed in white from head to toe looked at me and said, "You are right in here." He pointed to an empty bed. How did he know who I was? What if I wasn't the one he thought I was? The resident must have seen a questioning look on my face and lightly placed his hand on my shoulder, guiding me into the very small, curtained cubby. "Everyone knows when an airway patient is arriving." I'm certain he was trying to reassure me, but it made me more anxious.

A nurse was next to me instantly as I stopped at the end of the bed. She started in on her routine questioning and preparation protocol. Before the resident left, he told me I was in good hands and he would see me in the OR shortly. The nurse removed the paper hospital gown from the patient goody bag and announced that I need to be in a cloth gown because of the laser being used in my surgery. She said she would be right back and rushed off to get the appropriate gown. This was all new to me; I had never had surgery before, and I felt scared and alone.

I found a pair of ugly brown socks in the bag and put them on, removed all my jewelry, and waited. Once I was fully dressed in surgery attire and tucked into the rolling bed, an IV was placed into my arm. As the minutes passed, I could feel tears welling in my eyes, not from pain but from my fear of the unknown. "Can I have something to calm me down a bit?" I was trying to be brave. "I'm sorry dear, but they need you wide awake and able to communicate when you get to the OR." The tears rolled down my face, but I didn't make a sound.

My bed was rolled into another holding area where I was able to see Sue and Pat for a few minutes. They were calm and reassuring. Sue told me she would bring the kids to visit me later that evening so they could see for themselves that I was just fine. We hugged again and then I was moved on to the OR. It was cold, colorless, sterile smelling, and scary. The quiet tears returned as I was placed in the center of the room on a narrow, hard table directly under very bright lights. The room was filled with equipment. I didn't know what anything was and wasn't about to ask. There must have been a dozen people moving about performing various tasks. Several things were attached to my body in one way or another, and I was swaddled tightly into a blanket and strapped down so that I could not move. I began to panic.

One of the men in the room stepped to my side, looked closely into my eyes, held my hand, and spoke to me in a calm, quite tone. He assured me that everything was going to be just fine, that all of the activity around me was completely normal, and that it wouldn't be long before they would be able to give me some good drugs so I could go to sleep. He wiped the tears from my cheeks and continued to hold my hand as he checked the monitors and talked with the anesthesiologist.

Dr. Kara and the resident appeared and stepped to my side, so I could see them. They talked with me, explained what was going to happen, asked if I had any questions, and reassured me I was in good hands. I looked into Dr. Kara's kind eyes. "I have to get back to my children. I'm the only parent they have, and I promised to come home." She touched my shoulder and smiled, "I know."

Everyone was in place and ready to begin. Surrounding me, they talked through the process one more time. I didn't want to hear it again. I was nervous and anxious, and the tears started again. The anesthesiologist leaned over so I could see his eyes as he talked to me. "The IV is only delivering saline right now. We can't give you any pain medicine for the tracheostomy because we are concerned about your trachea collapsing. We need you awake and alert so you can communicate with us. As soon as the incision is made and the trachea is stabilized we'll push some drugs through your IV and put a mask over your face. You'll drift off to sleep and when you wake up, you won't remember anything." I shook my head, indicating that I understood.

My body began to shake uncontrollably. "Are you cold?" the resident asked me. I shook my head no. "Are you scared?" I nodded in the affirmative. He patted my leg, smiled, and said, "Okay, let's get this done so you can go to sleep." The belts were tightened around me, including the one holding my head in place, and my neck was extended. I couldn't move yet the shaking continued. The resident told me when he was about to make the incision into my neck. I felt the pressure of the knife as it sliced into my skin and the warm dripping sensation of liquid running down my neck. The doctor continued his narrative while he cut through tissue, moved my thyroid out of the way, and stabilized my larynx. I was afraid to close my eyes. I needed to have some kind of human connection, and at that moment all I had was eye contact from the man holding my hand. Someone from behind a white surgical mask explained it was time for me to go to sleep. Some medication was pushed through my IV, and I was told to take a few deep breaths through the clear mask being pressed against my face.

When I woke up, I couldn't talk. I was connected to more tubes and lines than I could count. I was still scared, and I wanted somebody, anybody, to be with me, to tell me I was okay.

Much later into the evening I was more alert and calmer, no

doubt thanks to the meds they were feeding me. Sue brought the kids to see me having first prepared them for what I looked like surrounded by all the medical equipment. They only stayed long enough for me to write them each a note saying I loved them and would be home soon. It was awful not being able to talk to them or hug them.

A week later I was released from the hospital and went home with the tracheostomy and cork around my neck. I could breathe through the tracheostomy, but if I wanted to talk, I had to put the cork into the hole and let air out through my mouth. The kids discovered that I could pop the cork out of the hole if I laughed, coughed, or sneezed, so, I became their entertainment. "Mom, pop your cork!" became the most requested activity in our home.

After a month with the tracheostomy, I was able to have it removed. I've never been so grateful for anything in my life. It was an awful experience. Unfortunately, my trachea issues continued and to date I have had 19 trachea surgeries but not another tracheostomy. Although my breathing is noisy, and I need to cough a lot to clear my airway of mucus, the good news is I can breathe on my own and am able to live a fairly normal life.

CHAPTER 20
FROM SURVIVING TO THRIVING

"When you stop focusing on what has been done to you, and take responsibility for your own life, you have all the power." – Patty Slupecki

Reflecting back on the course of events over the last, almost 16 years, I've discovered that I'm stronger than I ever gave myself credit for. I survived the entire first year in nearly complete numbness and with very little memory intact. Time wasn't measured by months or years but by one-day cycles lived without Mark. By the second year, the numbness had turned to tingling, and I became more aware of my unsettled life. I began purposefully changing our traditions and routines to detach from the memories we had with Mark and tried creating new memories for our lonely family of three. Year three was all about finding the correct diagnosis for my breathing issue. The next several years, I was just trying to get through the days, one at a time. I often survived by drinking myself to sleep. It was the only way I could put an end to painful days. Waking up the next morning was a disappointment. My unwanted reality was back...until I could go to sleep again.

Those early years were all about survival. I was learning how to live a new life as an only parent, sole provider, and household caretaker. Dealing with a dead bird in the yard, a dirty furnace filter, and a flooded basement became my responsibility alone. I gave the kids every material possession and travel experience I could, trying to make up for the fact they didn't have their dad any more. With each decision I made, I took the path of least resistance. I had to in order to keep myself functioning and moving through time, yet I wasn't moving *forward* in life. My charge was to raise my children; this was my only focus and guided all my choices. I didn't see past getting my kids to adulthood.

As time went by, happier moments began to outweigh the sad ones, but I continued to play the victim of my circumstances, blaming, or justifying, situations and actions on widowhood and being the only parent. I believed that my life had been taken from me and that I would never find another life I could truly enjoy. I felt as though I were condemned to an existence that I did not choose, deserve, or want. I was stuck with a major case of 'poor me.'

I dated and was even engaged twice believing I needed a partner to complete my life and make me happy. In both cases, I called it off and finally began searching for a way to be happy on my own. It wasn't what I wanted, but I also didn't want to just survive life any more. I wanted a life where I could be okay with myself and embrace a life worth living alone.

I read books, went to seminars and conferences, and researched how to get myself unstuck from grief and feeling sorry for myself. This began my journey of self-discovery. With each new lesson learned, I thought I had it all figured out and readjusted my life accordingly. As I'm sure you've guessed, I did *not* have it all figured out. Each lesson was a dot along my journey waiting to connect to the next.

It was about eight years into my widowhood when I finally

learned and acknowledged the fact that I needed to change my mindset and outlook on life. The question was how.

It took me another seven years of trial and error, victories and defeats, before I landed in a really good place. When I stopped focusing on what had been done *to* me or taken *from* me and took responsibility for my own life I was able to see that I'm the one with all the power. Everything in life is a choice, and I have the freedom and ability to choose the life I want.

What I want to tell you is that I never stopped trying; I never gave up on finding happiness, contentment, and a life worth living. It most certainly was a long and winding road, and I often found myself lost along the way. However, I eventually gathered the courage to chart a new course and learn a new route.

Today I'm exactly where I want to be. I look for and find the silver lining in all situations. I can be annoyingly positive to those who know me well. Through much soul searching, I rediscovered my passion for writing and dream of being an author. I'm following my heart and sharing my story in hopes of easing the pain for others. I strive to be authentically me, flaws and imperfections exposed. I have found true happiness with myself and am content with my life just as it is. After my nearly 16-year battle, I've made the move from surviving to thriving.

While I'm incredibly proud of how far I've come in my journey of self-discovery. I'm also humbled knowing there will always be more to learn. And for that, I am grateful.

Quotes

"Always say goodbye. Always say 'I love you'. One day, it will be the last moment you share with your loved one. Be sure you can look back on it with a smile." – Patty Slupecki

"People, things, and situations are put in front of us to serve a purpose. Be open to receiving a message or a lesson." – Patty Slupecki

"You can withstand much more than you ever thought possible. Yes, you can!"
– Patty Slupecki

"When you place your focus outside yourself, the impossible somehow becomes possible." – *Patty Slupecki*

"Lean on those willing to stand firm for you." – *Patty Slupecki*

"Acknowledgement of a Higher Power, the Universe, Source, or God brings a level of comfort only available through faith." – *Patty Slupecki*

"There are no perfect moms." – *Patty Slupecki*

"It's okay to be mad at God. It's okay to question Him. It's okay to yell and place blame. In time, a new level of faith will be understood." – Patty Slupecki

"It's okay if you don't know what to say or what to do at a visitation or funeral, just be there. Your presence means more than you will ever know."
– *Patty Slupecki*

"Signs are all around us, if we choose to see them!"– *Patty Slupecki*

"Give freely of yourself, your time, and your resources to those in need without the expectation of acknowledgment." – *Patty Slupecki*

"Grief is a journey that each of us must walk in our own way, in our own time."

— *Patty Slupecki*

"There are no coincidences. Every dot along our journey connects to the next."

— *Patty Slupecki*

"There is nothing more amazing or powerful than learning to control your thoughts. When you control your thoughts, you control your life."

— *Patty Slupecki*

"There is no better example of unconditional love than the love of a dog for his people."

— *Patty Slupecki*

"Holding on to negative emotions keeps you stuck. Choosing to let go of negative emotions frees you to move forward."   *- Patty Slupecki*

"Small, thoughtful gestures can often be more meaningful and memorable than the most grandiose shows of kindness." — Patty Slupecki

"Listen to your own body; it tells you everything you need to know." — Patty Slupecki

"You are capable of reaching heights greater than your wildest dreams have ever imagined." — Patty Slupecki

*"When you stop focusing on what has been done **to** you, and take responsibility for your own life, **you** have all the power n life." – Patty Slupecki*

"It's the people that really matter. Everything else is superficial." – Patty Slupecki

ABOUT THE AUTHOR

Patty Slupecki is an author, coach, speaker, and grief survivor. Widowed at 37 and left to raise her children alone, Patty struggled through crippling grief and depression. Unwilling to give up on life and remaining positive, she embarked on a journey of survival, self-development, and recovery. Patty uses her experience to help other widows navigate the unknown following the death of a spouse or life partner. It is her passion to offer hope and guidance along the road to a new normal.

Join Patty Slupecki's Social Community

www.pattyslupecki.com
f @pattyslupecki
t @pattyslupecki

FREE BONUS MATERIAL

How to Help the Grieving
A Checklist for Family, Friends, Neighbors, and Coworkers

Get exclusive insights and practical information for helping when someone experiences the death of a loved one.

✓ Learn what to say and what NOT to say.

✓ Understand what is helpful and what is harmful.

✓ Overcome the uncomfortableness that surrounds death.

✓ Gain confidence with funeral etiquette.

To download the Free Bonus Checklist, visit:

WWW.PATTYSLUPECKI.COM/BONUSMATERIAL

Join Patty Slupecki's Social Community

www.pattyslupecki.com
f @pattyslupecki
t @pattyslupecki